NOTES

ON THE

CULTIVATION OF CHORAL MUSIC

AND THE

ORATORIO SOCIETY OF NEW YORK

BY

H. E. KREHBIEL

AMS PRESS
NEW YORK

Reprinted from a copy in the collections of the
Westminster Choir College Library
Reprinted from the edition of 1884, New York
First AMS EDITION published 1970
Manufactured in the United States of America

International Standard Book Number: 0-404-03782-8
Library of Congress Number: 75-137315

AMS PRESS INC.
NEW YORK, N.Y. 10003

INTRODUCTION.

IT is not the purpose of this little book to give a complete history of the singing societies of New York City. That would be an unprofitable if not an impossible task. I had designed, originally, to write only a sketch of the Society which now represents our highest attainment in choral culture. Knowing, however, that an institution like the Oratorio Society could only be the outcome of many experiments in the past, and that its peculiar features and the cause of its present success could only be understood and valued if viewed as the fruit of early experiences, I addressed myself to a study of choral history in New York with the aim of bringing to the attention of the reader the influences which have been at work in the development of the present state of culture in this department of music. I was the more willing to let the record of my observations and speculations crowd my original purpose into the background, since I became more and more convinced, as I went on, that many others must have felt with me the need of some handy notes on choral culture. It is one of the inexplicable things in the literature of music, that we should be without a history of the rise and progress of amateur singing societies. It would be difficult, I am sure, to point to another influence in the history of modern music so fruitful in results to the art itself, as well as to its cultivators, as that exercised by voluntary organizations of amateur choristers; and its interest as a theme for discussion is greatly enhanced by the fact that the story is almost compassed by the present century, and its elements might, therefore, be got together with comparative ease. The cultivation of choral music in the phase in which it shows itself now in the great festivals of England, Germany, and America, and in the concerts of such choirs as the Handel and Haydn Society, of Boston, the Oratorio Society, of New York, and the choir of the Musical Festival Association, of Cincinnati, is less than a hundred years old; and a more exhaustive investigation than is possible here, owing to the narrow limits of this book, might flatter patriotic pride by discovering that American cities were quite as prompt as Berlin in giving it encouragement, though, it is true, under far less favorable circumstances.

The singing societies of Germany, by their diffusion of knowledge concerning the masterpieces of choral composition, and their nurture of a warm interest in music, were, beyond question, the most potent of the factors employed in the work of lifting that country to the eminence which it now occupies in music. The composers of the Viennese School of the eighteenth century wrested the supremacy from Italy by the virtue that lay in the freshness, vigor, and richness of their creations; these creations became the models for the succeeding generations, and the composers became the musical law-givers; but for the cultivation of the national musical spirit which established the conservatories, orchestras, and choirs, in which artists were educated in a manner that enabled them to maintain its proud supremacy, Germany rested, in a great measure, upon the impulse which went out from the crówning achievement of Fasch, the accompanist at the Court of Frederick the Great, of Prussia. To-day there are in the country that gave birth to this movement, three hundred cities and towns with singing societies and orchestras engaged in performing the best music written. This one fact ought to be argument enough to persuade some historian or critic to undertake the work suggested.

The history of singing societies in New York, shows all the efforts of two generations or more to have been afflicted with some weakness, organic or otherwise, which prevented the stability which has been one of the marked characteristics of the leading German choirs. Some of the predecessors of the Oratorio Society had fairly long, and certainly honorable, careers; but the first discovery of a retrospective glance is a confusion of enthusiastic beginnings and lame endings. Frequently the incentive to organization was not altogether laudable; often the foundation was unstable at the outset; in a wofully large number of cases dissolution was the result of controversies so silly that it would be a humiliation to be obliged to discuss them. Dissensions among the singers have been the cause of shipwreck quite as often as jealousies and petty squabbles in the management. Dr. F. L. Ritter, himself concerned in a number of the choral organizations

of New York City a score of years ago, discuss-
ing the causes of the want of permanence in the
societies now dead, notices these quarrels in his
book on "Music in America," and describes them
and their effect in these words:

One clique, instigated by some ambitious, half-educated
solo-singer, who wished to monopolize the solo parts all
through a season, or a candidate for some office (which
possibly gave the incumbent some influence in the coun-
sels of the society), would endeavor to put out another
clique that had so far managed the affairs of the society. Such an uncalled-for revolution very often thinned
the ranks of the members; or, the public performances
having been badly patronized, (this) would cause a
threatening deficit in the treasury, and the unwelcome
prospect would suddenly have an injurious effect upon
the voices of many sweet-throated members. Singing,
under such circumstances, was at once considered a
very unhealthy occupation, and so some of the choristers
found it necessary to take a vacation until the possible
return of more prosperous times.

As a rule, the increase in the number of societies has been accomplished much in the manner
in which some of the lowest order of animals reproduce their species — by self-division; and it
must be confessed that frequently the new organism was as ill-equipped for the battle of life as
the tenderest annelid. A study of these things
can not fail to throw an interesting side-light
upon the story of our present societies, and

hence, so far as was practicable, a glance at the record of past efforts in the line of choral cultivation has been given in the following pages. The discussion is, however, not intended to include the small secular choirs and glee clubs of which there are now a number in the city, nor the Chorus Society, which has grown up within the last three years, nor even the distinctively German societies, whose activity has occasionally been extended into the province in which the mission of the Oratorio Society lies. Though worthy of record, the story of these organizations is not essential to the present discussion, which is, of necessity, limited in its scope. When the development, in this country, of music in any of its forms is discussed, however, expression should be given to the obligation which America is under to the German element of its population, which, for the last fifty years, has been a most persistent and most admirable impulsive force. A sentence in my "Account of the Fourth Musical Festival, held at Cincinnati in 1880," touching the origin of music festivals in this country in the German love for part-songs by male voices, gives expression to this truth, and I

reproduce it as a deserved tribute to the influence of the German-Americans in promoting our
national musical culture :

When the German came, he brought with him his
loves. To them he is as true as Hero to Leander. The
traditions which have been fixed in his nature through
centuries of national growth are not shaken by a change
in his surroundings. He crosses the ocean, but the
music of the Rhine's murmur, the song of the Lorelei,
lives in his heart; he makes his home on the western
prairie, but still is within the shadow of the Brocken
and the Schwarzwald. He carries his country and his
country's song with him, and so soon as he finds the
congenial companionship which he loves, the institutions
of his fatherland are established. Prominent among them
is the *Männergesang*. It is a very natural outgrowth of
the German's love for song and companionship. It cele-
brates the things nearest his heart—his love, his country,
nature, friendship, and sociability. He is born and bred
in the love of these things, and so soon as he is able
to comprehend anything, they are instilled into his nature
through the potent medium of the *Volkslieder*—little songs
which, with simple sentiments and tuneful melodies, both
the fruits of truest inspiration, create and nourish the
loves of his race.

H. E. K.

NEW YORK, MAY, 1884.

I.

ONE hundred and fourteen years ago, Dr. Burney made a tour of France and Italy, to collect materials for his "General History of Music." Two years later, still bent on the same mission, he visited Germany, the Netherlands, and the United Provinces, perambulating through these countries as he had done through France and Italy, with eyes and ears wide open, an eager note-book in hand, and plainly possessed by a forefather of that quizzical demon popularly supposed nowadays to be the inspiration of the newspaper interviewer. Indeed, his purposes were very like those of the modern newspaper correspondent—he was searching for information, and he wanted to get it at first hand. "It is well known," he wrote afterwards, in his introduction to the record of his second tour, "that such merchandise as is capable of adulteration is seldom genuine after passing through many hands; and this principle is still more generally allowed with respect to intelligence, which is, perhaps, never pure but at the source." And later he adds, in justification of his peripatetic plan, "for if knowledge be medicine for the soul, according to the famous inscription on the Egyptian Library, it seems as much to concern us to obtain it genuine as to procure unadulterated medicine

11

for the body"—an argument which can scarcely be controverted.

Never was a search for unsophisticated intelligence prosecuted with more diligence and energy than that of this musical historian. He was in possession of a magical sesame in the shape of letters from a powerful friend in the British nobility, and all doors swung open at his approach. He visited the libraries and examined their treasures; conversed with almost every then living musician of eminence; visited the theaters like the most inveterate and confirmed of pleasure-seekers; worshiped in the cathedrals like the most devout of Catholics; attended services in the churches like the most pious of Lutherans, and went up into the synagogues like a Jew in whom there was no guile. He did not always note the words of the preacher's text, but he seldom omitted a memorandum on the tone and compass of the organ and the taste and skill of the organist. The record of his tour, when written out and printed, filled three volumes which, by Dr. Johnson's own confession, became the model of the latter's "Tour to the Hebrides." The volumes pictured the then state of music in the countries visited, and they have remained till to-day the delight of musical students, as much for the honest and straightforward style of the recital, as for the vast number of significant and suggestive facts which are marshalled in their pages. Occasionally, there comes a sentence which provokes a smile, because of its naïve satisfaction with a state which, in the light of to-day, looks like the infancy of modern music, and its innocence of all premonition of the morn that was just breaking. It is not only amusing, but also a little surprising, for instance, that when Mozart was already sixteen years of age, Dr. Burney should make room in his book for an extract from a letter, which, speaking of the young musician who had long ago outgrown his prodigy years, contained a sentence like this: "If I may judge of the music which I heard of his composition in the orchestra, he is one further instance of early fruit being more extraordinary than excellent." The sincerity of Dr. Burney, however, and his devotion to the truest and best art of his time, are so obvious that the smile called out by so short-sighted an observation never becomes derisive.

That instrumental music was in its swaddling clothes four generations ago, is plain from Dr. Burney's notes on the theatrical orchestras, and court and military bands, which he listened to in the big and little towns of the Continent. In only one phase had it reached a plane comparable with that of to-day—in the composition and performance of pieces for the organ. In organ music change is slow, partly because of the nature of the instrument, partly because of its early mechanical development. A more significant fact is that which appears not from what Dr. Burney says, but from what he does

not say—the fact which concerns our present inquiry—
namely, that one hundred and fourteen years ago there
was not in all musical Europe a single amateur choral
society. As a matter of historical fact, it was only
ninety-six years ago that the first public singing society
composed of amateurs was established. This is something that ought not to be overlooked when the history
of choral music is being reviewed, as its significance
can hardly be overestimated. Singing societies, beyond
question, exert the most powerful of all influences in
the promotion of musical culture, not only in a community, but also in the individual member. Schumann
recognized this when, in his "*Musikalische Haus- und
Lebens-Regeln,*" he set down the admirable advice: "Sing
diligently in choirs, particularly the middle voices.
This will make you musical;" and Thibaut, in his
truly classical little work on purity in music ("*Ueber
Reinheit der Tonkunst*"), gives it admirable expression in
the words: "*Ist von Erhebung und Veredlung des Ge-
müths durch die Musik die Rede, so verdienen gewiss die
Singvereine den ersten Platz.   Denn wenn die Tonsetzer
durch herrliche Worte begeistert waren, so hatte diess auf
ihre Compositionen den sichtbarsten Einfluss; und was
vergleicht sich der menschlichen Stimme, wenn edle Ge-
danken die Seele des Sängers bewegen?*" The sentence
sounds like an utterance of Plato. Herman Kretsch-
mar, in a monograph recently published in Germany,

gives an admirable *resumé* of the advantages which accrue from singing societies.

We owe it to them [he says] that a serious spirit is again become dominant in music; and they give the strongest protection against the encroachments of that superficial enjoyment which is the product of the modern system of concert-giving, by confronting that great portion of the public whose relation to our masterpieces is confined to a passing hearing, with a band of persons who are accustomed, through diligence, profound study, and enthusiasm, to reach the significance of the music. Yet as much as art profits by the singing societies, and notwithstanding that through their influence it has entered upon a new phase of life, the greatest good accrues to the members themselves. In no other art are amateurs privileged to enjoy the spiritual beauties of a creation in the degree that music offers to choristers. Whoever belongs to a singing society in which the study is well conducted, at each performance accomplishes a work and receives an artistic reward analogous to that of the painter who has copied a masterpiece. And he who has spent a generation in such a society can cherish his recollections like an entire museum. How securely such an owner can hold his treasures is shown by those choristers who, at an annual performance of the "Ninth Symphony," or the "St. Matthew Passion," sing their parts without the book; and how comprehensive it is possible to make such a collection we can learn from a glance at the career of twenty-five years of one of the best amateur choirs in Germany—the *Riedel'sche Verein*, in Leipsic. In its programmes we find eighty-odd compositions of the German school, from Tannhäuser and Schütz down to the newest names of Brahms, Liszt, and Cornelius. Bach is represented in one hundred and two concerts, six times with the B Minor Mass; Beethoven ten times, with the "Missa Solemnis." The foreign com-

posers are all comprehended in this repertory so far as
they have significant merit, from Josquin to Berlioz,
great and small, beside Palestrina and Lassus a Porpora
and Claudin Le Jeune. That such a treasure of the
loftiest art-works extending with equal justice over all
nations, times, and tendencies, should be confided by a
small circle of *cognoscenti* to a few hundred collaborators
and their friends, and then delivered over to the intellectual property of a whole city, is one of the wonders
of modern times. In your singing societies you possess
a magic power which, it is to be hoped, will have the
most benevolent nurture through all futurity.

The occasion of this utterance was a celebration,
by the *Riedel'sche Verein*, of its twenty-fifth anniversary,
in 1879, and though the remarks apply with peculiar
force to Germany, the cradle and the true home of
choral organizations, they have likewise significance
here and elsewhere. What the cultivation of Handel's
music in England has done for that country is not to
be measured, and the fact that in the manufacturing
towns of Great Britain thousands of men and women
might be assembled on a day's notice to sing "The
Messiah" without the notes, tells more of the gentle-
ness and refinement of the working classes in that
country than hundreds of learned essays on social
science.

Another accomplishment of singing societies lies in
this: They supplied the factor which revived the de-
caying interest in the masterpieces of the greatest composers, Bach and Handel in especial, by giving them

the adequate expression which they had lacked from the time of their creation. When Bach and Handel wrote their Passions, Church Cantatas, and Oratorios they could only dream of such majestic performances as those works receive now; and it is one of the miracles of art that they should have written in so masterly a manner for forces that they could never hope to control. Who would think, when listening to the "Hallelujah!" of "The Messiah," or the great double choruses of "Israel in Egypt," in which the voice of the composer is "as the voice of a great multitude, and as the voice of many waters, and as the voice of many thunderings, saying, Alleluia, for the Lord God Omnipotent reigneth!" that these colossal compositions were never heard by Handel from any chorus larger than the most modest of our church choirs? A few notes from old records tell plainer than argument how vast has been the change made by the establishment of amateur singing societies with reference to the performance of these compositions.

At the last performance of "The Messiah" at which Handel was advertised to appear (it was for the benefit of his favorite charity, the Foundling Hospital, on May 3, 1759; he died before the time, however), the singers, including principals, numbered twenty-three, while the instrumentalists numbered thirty-three. At the first great Handel Commemoration, in Westminster Abbey, in 1784, the choir numbered two hundred and seventy-five, the band two hundred and fifty; and this was the most numerous force ever gathered together for a single performance in England up to that time. In 1791 the Commemoration was celebrated by a choir of five hundred and a band of three hundred and seventy-five. In May, 1786, Johann Adam Hiller, one of Bach's successors as Cantor of the St. Thomas School, in Leipsic, directed what was termed a "*Massenaufführung*" of "The Messiah" in the Domkirche, in Berlin. His "masses" consisted of one hundred and eighteen singers and one hundred and eighty-six instrumentalists. In Handel's operas, and sometimes even in his oratorios, the *tutti* meant, in his time, little more than a union of all the solo singers; and even Bach's Passion music and church cantatas, which seem as much designed for numbers as the double choruses of "Israel," were rendered in the St. Thomas Church by a ludicrously small choir. Of this fact a record is preserved in the archives of Leipsic. In August, 1730, Bach submitted to the authorities a plan for a church choir of the pupils in his care. In this plan his singers numbered twelve, there being one principal and two ripienists in each voice; with characteristic modesty he barely suggests a preference for sixteen. The circumstance that in the same document he asked for at least eighteen instrumentalists (two more if flutes were used), taken in connection with the figures given relative to "The Messiah" performances, gives an insight into the relations between the vocal and the instrumental parts of a choral performance in those days.

It must be remembered that throughout England, Germany, France, and Italy, in the last century, chorus singing was still in the hands of professional singers in church, school, or institute choirs (organizations like the Chapel Royal of England), or the choristers of the theatres. Under such circumstances a command of really numerous forces was out of the question, and it is when we contrast an oratorio performance of to-day with one of those earlier days that we realize for the first time how great was the revolution accomplished by the new movement which had its inception in the founding of the Berlin *Singakademie*, the forerunner of the thousands of singing societies which are to be found all over the Occidental world to-day.

II.

KARL Friedrich Christian Fasch, the founder of the
Singakademie, historically the first of the amateur singing societies, was a musician in the service of
Frederick tì Great, of Prussia, the royal flute player.
His position when, as a young man, he entered that
famous monarch's employ, was that of assistant to Philip
Emanuel Bach, with whom he used to alternate every
four weeks in the task of playing the cembalo to the
King's daily exercises on the flute. For a time, in
later years, he directed the Royal Opera, and that he
retained still the favor of the monarch who was wont
to exercise the same vigilance and enforce the same
strict discipline over his musical servants that he did
over his military, is as much a tribute to Fasch's skill
as a courtier as to his excellence as a musician. For
Frederick the Great's musical taste, knowledge, and
skill were not of a mean order, notwithstanding that
his favorite instrument was the flute. Fasch's whole
artistic life, though he outlived his first royal master,
was spent in the service of the Prussian Court, and
though he suffered more than his share of disappointments in the matters of preferments and rewards, he
never sacrificed his artistic ideals or stooped to anything that disgraced his manhood. He was weak in

body and somewhat eccentric in habits, particularly in the lines in which he sought relaxation from his professional labors, mixing in a singular manner the study of medicine, geography, and naval warfare with the invention and construction of card houses, but nevertheless a man of serious purposes and profound musical learning, and especially devoted to the strict style of *a capella* composition and those contrapuntal ·lzzles which used to be the delight of musical scholiasts. Among his achievements in composition was a monstrous canon in twenty-five parts. It was a manifestation of this devotion which, in the first instance, led to the step which gave a new phase to the cultivation of choral music.

In 1783 Reichardt, the Royal Chapelmaster, returning from a visit to Italy, brought to Berlin, among other musical curiosities, a mass in sixteen parts composed by Orazio Benevoli. He lent the score to Fasch, who, struck with the work, copied it in full. The episode turned Fasch's thoughts back to an old channel. The mass of the Italian master had been composed one hundred and seventy years before. In transcribing it, Fasch found errors and weaknesses which led him to think that he could also write a mass in sixteen parts, and carry the parts out strictly in four choruses, which Benevoli had not done. "He wanted, perhaps," says his pupil and affectionate biographer, Zelter (Mendelssohn's teacher), "to create a work from which, one hun-

dred and seventy years after, a connoisseur might see
that there had also been a German harmonist who had
essayed a composition in sixteen parts and succeeded."
He finished the mass in a few weeks, working so hard
at it as to bring on a hemorrhage of the lungs.
Then he wanted to hear it. He tried it with twenty
of the royal singers in Potsdam, but the experiment
was a failure; the effect was not what he had fondly
imagined it. He tried it again, this time in church,
with singers from the choirs, but he feared to tax them
with rehearsals, and the second experiment was disap-
pointing. The circumstance undoubtedly opened the
eyes of the musician to the need of a society capable
of singing church music written in the classic manner.

The story has become universal, that Fasch's desire
to hear his mass worthily performed was the motive for
the organization of the *Singakademie.* This is not
borne out, however, by Zelter's recital. It was six
years after the disappointments connected with the mass
that the seed was planted which has borne the wonderful fruit of which we have spoken.

In 1789 there was among Fasch's pupils a Mademoi-
selle Charlotte Dieterich, a step-daughter of the Privy-
Councillor Milow. She belonged to that class of musical
amateurs who are the salt of the artistic earth. It was
her custom, at about the date mentioned, to gather a
few of the music lovers from her circle of friends into
her home of an evening and devote the time to singing

part-songs. Fasch was the accompanist. He grew interested in the gatherings and composed music for the zealous band, that grew more and more numerous with each month. In 1791 the circle, who now met regularly once a week for study under Fasch, numbered twenty persons, among whom were a few professional singers who looked upon music as something better than a trade. In 1792 the number had increased to thirty and included virtuosi of the highest rank. The salons of the Privy-Councillor Milow were now too small for the meetings, and the choir made bold to apply to the curators of the Royal Academy of Science and Art for a meeting-room in the Academy. The application received the favor of the curators, and this fact bringing with it a need of organization, the choir took a name, established a system of dues, appointed officers, and the famous *Singakademie* entered upon its public career. In 1793 it numbered fifty-five members; in 1794, sixty-four (and now friends were admitted to its performances); in 1796, eighty-three, and at the end of 1797, one hundred and forty-eight, who represented the four voices in the following proportions: seventy sopranos, twenty-eight contraltos, twenty-four tenors, and twenty-six basses.

The government of the society was vested by Fasch in a presiding council of three men and three women; he himself retained full power in the musical administration, and it was upon his nomination that the council was chosen. He gave his services as director gratuitously, and not only this, but also his labor as composer; he even copied the parts for all the singers and paid his share of the dues, which were fixed at half a *thaler* per month, until the growth of the society made this unnecessary. When the choir was fairly launched Fasch quit all private instruction and devoted himself almost exclusively to the new work. He composed motets and psalms without number, copied and multiplied the parts not only of these, but also of the compositions of other masters, and enlisted in a wonderful degree the interest of contemporary musicians. Reichardt, Naumann, and Himmel composed admirable works for the choir, and the library, which grew rapidly because of Fasch's untiring and self-sacrificing zeal and energy, soon contained besides these, a large number of the works of Johann Sebastian Bach, Durante, Leo, Handel, Cannicciani, Benevoli, Graun, Hasse, Palestrina, Marcello, Mozart, Schulz, Kirnberger, Allegri, and other German and Italian masters. It is recorded by Zelter, who, after Fasch's death, succeeded to the directorship of the *Singakademie*, not without a little glow of pride in the accomplishment of his revered teacher, that so admirable was the administration of the society's affairs, that by a slight increase of the dues in the fall of 1796, it became possible to provide carriages for the lady members through the winter months, so that inclement weather did not prevent the gathering of a full choir.

In the purity of its aims, the zeal with which it prosecuted them, and the harmonious spirit which pervaded all its doings, the *Singakademie* has remained a model for all singing societies up to the present time, and it is pleasant to be able to trace some parallels between the devotion of its members and that of the original promoters of the Oratorio Society, as well as to note that in the latter the musical system of the former has been perpetuated.

III.

THE seeds that produced our singing societies were brought to New York, not from the older settlements of New England, but from Europe. What was the character and condition of the soil into which these seeds fell? Originally bare and stony, it must be confessed. The earliest and most vigorous influence in the social development of New York, was Dutch, notwithstanding the brevity of the time during which the town remained under the political dominion of the Netherlands. The customs of the place, the tastes of its people, the character of its entertainments were swayed by the Dutch element until far into the eighteenth century. The town was captured by the English in 1664; fifteen years later there was only one Episcopal minister in New York, who read the service in the Dutch church Sundays after the departure of the Dutch congregation; and it was not until 1693 that English influence was powerful enough to secure a charter for Trinity Church, though the effort was begun some years before. Under such a social *régime* there was little hope for music. The first colonists were anything but artistically minded, and a century after the English had taken possession of Nieuw Amsterdam little other music was encouraged in old Amsterdam than "the jingling of bells and of ducats."

The stolid Dutch burghers, even when well-to-do, cared little for "concourse of sweet sounds," and we can not think it entirely insignificant that after the colony had outlived its first privations, and merriment had asserted its claims, the pleasure parties that drove out to Haarlem to dance had to depend for inspiration upon the fiddle of a negro slave. The fact is, that the first colonists, under the Dutch government, were mostly poor adventurers, who were too much engrossed with the pursuit of money to give much concern to any kind of mental culture. The colony was without a clergyman or schoolmaster twelve years.

Besides all this, nothing is truer than that this phase of musical culture roots in the Church; and in the case of the early settlers of New York, the influence exerted in this direction by the Church was restrictive instead of encouraging. A large contingent of the colonists were French Huguenots, and they, like the Dutch, were members of the Reformed Church. This Church, two hundred years ago, was as seriously determined as the Puritans of England a little later to extinguish every spark of the artistic element in religious service. When the Genevan Psalter was adopted, Calvin gave the strictest injunction that neither its words nor its melodies were to be altered. In the then excited condition of the religious mind the restraining influence of such an injunction, and of an expression like that which follows, had a power which we can hardly estimate to-day.

"Those songs and melodies," said Calvin, "which are composed for the mere pleasure of the ear, and all they call ornamental music, and songs for four parts, do not behoove the majesty of the Church, and can not fail greatly to displease God." It is true that, in time, Goudimel's harmonies found their way into the Dutch Reformed Church, but Goudimel himself was careful, when he published them, to state that the three parts which he had added to the old psalm tunes were not designed for use in the church, "but for the enjoyment of God at home." There is nothing new under the sun. Superstitious veneration for a primitive form once looked upon as efficacious, and superstitious fear of the consequences which might follow the change of a note or syllable, restricted the religious chant of the ancient Egyptians, led the fathers of the Christian Church to inveigh against musical instruments, and still persuades the Scotch Presbyterian Church to taboo organs.

This is a phenomenon which has received so little attention in the books that I can not refrain from considering it more fully, even at the cost of a digression which may interrupt my narrative for a space. I am led into the consideration by a discovery from reading and conversation with persons familiar with musical history, that the one-sided character of our text-books, in which the early stages of the instrumental art are all but ignored, has led to an imperfect conception of the influence of religion and the Church in musical development. Our music is spoken of in all the handbooks as peculiarly a product of Christianity, and no fact in its history is more widely known than that the regulation and preservation of the art is due to the Christian Church. With this view I have no quarrel; my purpose is only to urge that, owing to the prominence which this fact assumes whenever a glance is taken into the past, and also, no doubt, because of the other circumstance that the first musical historians, like the first musical law givers, were children of the Church, who viewed the world and all its activities from the narrow windows of their cloister cells, another influence of great potency has suffered sad neglect. This influence is that which came from without the temple walls —the profane influence—to which is due a great deal of credit for the development of the art as we have it to-day. The free spirit which developed instrumental music was developed by the people in spite of the Church; and when the aid of instruments was called in to heighten the effect of the vocal art, the marriage was celebrated, not as a religious rite, but as a civil compact. It was the attempt to revive the Greek tragedy in the Italian opera which, under the dispensation of Christianity, first brought about a combination of voices and instruments of significance to the future of both branches.

The debt that all the arts owe to religion is universally acknowledged; and it need not be denied that music is the principal debtor. The legends of almost all classical peoples ascribe to music a divine origin, and thus give evidence that, already in primitive times, it was set apart as a proper and potent means of worship. We shall see how natural was this selection if we but consider how closely music is related to our inner nature. It was not necessary for man to have an articulate language before feeling, that is, before becoming conscious of, the effect produced upon him by natural phenomena; but it was necessary that he should have medium of expression for that feeling when it came. The sigh and moan that speak of sorrow; the ringing shout that publishes joy— these must have been as unvolitional in primitive man as they are in us. So long as man remained a savage, in intelligence raised but little above the brute, we can im- agine him uttering his exclamations when affected either by triumph or by defeat, by joy or by sorrow; but we cannot imagine him, I take it, making any studied and specific use of the tones which he had thus involuntarily discovered. Even the imitative faculty could, at that time, have had but little exercise; for his thoughts and ambitions ran no higher than to provide physical com- fort. As man grew in civilization, however, and finer feelings were aroused within him by his associations with his kind, and by his observations of the terrible and beautiful phenomena of nature, there came, very natu- rally, a rude religious worship, with which he sought to appease the supernatural powers by which he found himself surrounded, and to testify his appreciation of those which he recognized as beneficial to him. For this worship he already had a language; awe, fear, reverence, on the one hand, and delight and satisfaction on the other, had found their tones. Religion, itself the offspring of man's inner nature, found its fittest language in that which came most direct from the emotions. Thus was originated the religious chant which, in the antique world, as in the later Christian, formed the germ from which was developed the musical art. The development of music was thus, in a great measure, linked with the development of religion; and the parallel is easily traceable in the history of the antique art. Among those peoples whose religion never rose above a gross form of idolatry, we find the religious chant restricted to a primitive rudeness; while amongst others (notably the Greeks, where there was an ever-working tendency to liberality in the form of worship, where contests of poets, rhapsodists, orators, actors, musicians, and gymnasts all made up part of the national religious system), the mission of music became wonderfully widened, and the pinnacle of its excellence under the antique *régime* was there attained. It was in Greece that music reached its highest excellence and its widest use, a circumstance which is accounted for by its broader culture and its greater liberality and ideality in religion. The restrictions which fettered the religious chant in countries where the primitive element of fear had remained the basis of the re-

ligion, were here lifted, and the result was the natural
one of a development of the whole art.

It must be remembered, however, that the Hellenic
ideal was one which steadily subordinated the emotional
to the rational element of man.   Music, therefore, was
not an independent art, but was subordinated to poetry.
The sensuous charm which lay in the tones themselves
was wedded to the wisdom expressed in the words of
the poet and philosopher; and this high type of a beautiful art, which united a power that compelled the sense
with another that persuaded the reason, was made an
instrument for the spread of religion and the virtues
which were next in importance to it—patriotism and
morality.   This accounts for the fact that, though instrumental music as a separate art was cultivated, it did not
receive the attention bestowed on the vocal art, which,
in the classic sense, was an infinitely higher form.   The
voice of instruments alone could never become the voice
of reason; and hence it was necessary that this branch
should be guarded jealously.   The story of the banish-
ment of Timotheus by the Spartan senate for having
added four strings to the *Kithara*, thus extending the
number of possible combinations, seems to me sufficient
proof that such was the view held by the Greek philoso-
phers of instrumental music.   But, if more were wanted,
it might be found in the writings of Plato, who carefully
prescribes the mode in which the youth of his ideal state
are to be instructed, interdicts others and certain instru-

ments because of their enervating character, and follows up the discussion of music with gymnastics, as if to provide at once an antidote for the art which, useful as it was, yet had a tendency to make man effeminate. It would seem, therefore, that wherever influences of the character described operated upon the art, we must look in another direction for the causes which effected a development of purely instrumental music.

When Christianity came to end the old and inaugurate the new dispensation in the affairs of the world, Rome had succeeded Greece as the center of civilization and political power. What had music to hope from Rome? Little, in the antique sense; much, as viewed from the point of view which we occupy to-day. For the promotion of the art which beautiful Greece had chosen as her model, while she was fashioner and director of all intellectual activity, nothing could be expected from Rome. "In Latium there was no national god of song," says Mommsen. Why? Simply because the Latins were never a poetical nor an artistic people from impulse. They were educated in the arts of war and not of peace; they were an unemotional, unspiritual, materialistic people, whose arts, laws, and religion sprang from nothing higher than the instincts which, combined with craft and power, laid the world in bondage at their feet, and gave them political and commercial supremacy. The central object of their worship was Mars, the killing god. "Their religion," says Mommsen, speaking of them at an early period of their national life, "was grounded mainly on man's enjoyment of earthly pleasures, and only in a subordinate degree on his fear of the wild forces of nature. It consisted pre-eminently, therefore, in expressions of joy, in lays and songs, in games and dances, and, above all, in banquets. In Italy the slaughter of cattle was at once a household feast and an act of worship; a pig was the most acceptable offering to the gods, just because it was the usual roast for a feast." Their religion never rose to a higher ideality. "A code of moral and ethical rules, furthering and preserving civil order and the pious relations within the state and family, were the palpable results of this religion, which, in its barrenness of metaphysical notions, did next to nothing for the furtherance of art,"—this is the characterization of the Roman religion when the nation was at its best, made by another writer. Such a religion was neither a conservator nor a promoter; it could not preserve the art legacy that came from Greece. The attitude of the Roman state toward music was one of toleration rather than protection. With the other arts (except poetry) its practice, while voted reputable, was left to the Greek slaves. The high educational purpose ascribed to it by the thinking Greeks was entirely ignored; it was only a luxury, fit accompaniment for feast and frolic, necessary adjunct of the lascivious dance. True to their selfish nature, the Romans sanctioned the native flute and condemned the lyre—the instrument of Marsyas was favored above that of Apollo. Trumpets and flutes, tipped with metal to render their tones louder and more aggressive, remained their favorite instruments till the downfall of the empire; they found in them the truest echoes of their national peculiarities; for, before they became warriors, the Latins were a pastoral people. During the reign of Nero, and one or two other emperors, a show of musical culture was made; but it partook only of the idle extravagance which characterized that age. The distinction between secular and religious music became less and less manifest as the religious festivals became more and more debased; the flutes which played in the funeral procession also played at the debauch. Then, as people after people were conquered and made subject to Rome, new gods were admitted by resolution to the freedom of the city; and soon all that might have remained of the primitive secrecy with regard to the religious chant passed away, and Rome, adopting the gods of the whole world, celebrated in public, with as many varieties of music, the worship of the Greek Dionysos, the Syrian Astarte, the Egyptian Isis, and deities innumerable from all parts of the earth.

Only a revulsion against the excesses of ancient Rome could have caused the Christian Church, when it came upon the scene, from profiting by the eclecticism in worship which characterized the Roman religion.

The primitive spirit of the new religion was in harmony
with its liberality, but obvious causes drove the Church
into conservatism.   Its musical service, at first perfectly
free, soon became infected with an element which
swayed the old system based on superstition and fear.
We know, for instance, that however lofty some of the
things in the Egyptian religion may have been, the
manifestations in the temple worship were of the rudest
kind.   The grandeur of the temple frequently enshrined
nothing better than a crocodile or a serpent, which dis-
ported its repulsive body upon cushions of royal purple.
Hymns were sung in its worship, but the spirit of those
hymns was like the spirit of the religion, primitive
and rude; the original dominion of fear was still present to restrain the development of the religious ideal
and, of course, the religious service.   The same
restrictive spirit operated against the development of
the temple music, and hence we find a record in
Plato's writings to the effect that the chants sung in the
Egyptian temples were at his time what they had been
for thousands of years, so long, indeed, that the priests
considered that they had been composed by Isis.   In
the nature of testimony corroborative of Plato's statement, is the quotation made from Demetrius by Herder
in his "*Aelteste Urkunde des Menschengeschlechts,*" to the
effect that the temple chant of the Egyptian priests consisted of a repetition, in regular and never-varying
order, of the seven sacred vowels of the language.

We have seen how the Greeks, though they had an instrumental art, restricted its development through fear of injury to their philosophical conception of the province of music—its subordination to thought. Had this not been in the way, and had they possessed the modern invention, harmony, there would have been nothing to prevent them from developing the perfect art which we have to-day through a union of both influences and both departments. The characterization made of the Roman practice showed that it tended to promote that form which appealed most to the senses and least to the higher ideals. When the Christian Church, therefore, began its work of establishment and regulation, though it admitted the service of song which bore unmistakable evidence of worldly influences, it turned with abhorrence from that art which had been chiefly in the sensual orgies of latter-day paganism. Instruments were excluded from the church, and their strong denunciation by the Church fathers created a prejudice which has not yet entirely vanished. How this step retarded musical progress would furnish a theme for much thought and profitable discussion. How much might not the monks have been aided in their laborious work of elaborating the rules of harmony had they been assisted by a harp of such admirable construction and evidently large capabilities as that which the English traveler, Bruce, found painted on the rocky walls of a burial vault in Egypt? But the prejudice and the fear which came a

heritage from the early religions caused the instruments
to be shut without the pale of the Church; and they
could not participate in the growth which was nourished
and promoted in the cloister cells and in the gorgeous
ceremonies which the Church borrowed from paganism.
To the people belonged the instruments; and, very naturally, they continued to be the publishers of those forms
which lived, not only independently of, but despite, the
Church—the popular dance tunes.

Their practitioners were a despised class. As late
as the fourteenth and fifteenth centuries, instrumentalists
were, in law, vagabonds. They had none of the rights
of citizenship; the religious sacraments were denied
them; their children were not permitted to inherit property or to learn an honorable trade; and after death
the property for which they had toiled escheated to the
Crown. In the old Chronicles of Europe there are
many singular regulations concerning them, not the
least ridiculous being one according to which the musical vagabond who had been injured by a reputable
citizen received, on appeal to a legal tribunal, the satisfactory privilege of beating the shadow of the ag-
gressor.

With the instruments the dance, too, had been de-
prived of its dignity; and it is interesting to see how
the despised ones united and, without the aid of religious influences, developed the homely dance tunes into
art forms of grand dimensions and noble designs, forms

which make possible the highest expression of the
beautiful in art—the suite, the sonata, and the symphony. After such an accomplishment the instrumental
art could no longer be overlooked; and during the last
century some of its sublimest utterances have been
given in the service of the Church.

I have taken the reader on a wide excursion, but I
trust he has found recompense in the light which the
facts adduced throw upon one of the stumbling blocks
which I have noted as lying in the way of choral culture in New York a century ago, and which could
only be removed by a change in the social and religious conditions of the city. It can be accepted, I
think, therefore, that it was not until the English influence became dominant in the community that the
phase of musical culture set in which could blossom
into amateur singing societies. Unfortunately we are
left in the dark as to the date of this beginning. Dr.
Ritter, in the chapter of his new book devoted to the
early musical societies of New York City, has this to
say about their genesis:*

Musical societies were established in New York about
the middle of the last century, and the Apollo Society
seems to have been the foremost among them. Others
followed and again disappeared. Thus at the beginning
of the third decade of this century the principal New
York musical societies were the New York Choral So-

---

* " Music in America," Charles Scribner's Sons, page 131.

ciety, the Philharmonic Society, the Euterpean, and a
Handel and Haydn Society, which had a brilliant but
short existence.

The Philharmonic Society referred to was not the
present notable institution, but a glee club, modelled
perhaps, after the numerous Glee Unions of Great
Britain. Unfortunately this is all that Dr. Ritter has
to say about the Apollo Club, set down as the foremost among the pioneer organizations in New York.
It would have been well if the statements in the para-
graph (which, if true, are of unique interest in musical
history) had not been left so vague and unsupported
by proofs. If musical societies, like some of those of
which Dr. Ritter's chapter treats, really were established in New York City "about the middle of the
last century," it might be possible to prove for New
York a priority in popular choral culture over the
cities of the Old World; for it is evident from what
has been set forth in the preceding chapters, that at
the time specified- Europe was practically without amateur singing societies, the cultivation of choral music
being left to the organized choirs of churches, hospitals,
asylums, and institutions of learning, and the singers
being professional choristers. It is not impossible, or
even improbable, that America really enjoyed the priority, and for this reason it is to be the more regretted
that Dr. Ritter, who devoted much time to the early
musical history of New York, Boston, and other Ameri-

can cities, did not find enough evidence to remove the
question outside the field of controversy. Necessity is
the mother of invention, and as amateur theatricals are
certain, in an amusement-loving community, to precede
the establishment of a play-house, musical performances
by amateurs were very likely to grow up in a new
country in which the institutions of the old had not
been transplanted. The musical culture of England in
the early part of the last century was of the most arti-
ficial kind. Not only the Italian opera, but also the
oratorio, was an aristocratic entertainment which seldom
condescended to divert and edify the masses, but remained a matter of fashion. *"But* Mufick *in this Age,"*
said John Playford in his "Introduction to the Skill of
Mufick," *"is in low efteem with the generality of People.
Our late and Solemn* Mufick, *both Vocal and Inftrumental,
is now juftled out of Efteem by the New Corants and Jigs
of Foreigners, to the Grief of all fober and judicious Un-
derftanders of that formerly folid and good* Mufick: *Nor
muft we expect Harmony in Peoples minds, fo long as
Pride, Vanity, Faction, and Difcords are fo predominant
in their Lives."* The "solid and good Musick," the
decay of which is here deplored, or what there was
left of it in public use, was monopolized by the trained
choirs of the Church, and until long after Handel's
time the participation of amateurs in any musical performance was practically confined to the psalmody of the
non-conformist Churches and the social singing of glees.

For their Church music Americans were thrown upon their own resources. In New England a zealous element among the Puritan clergy began, as early as the middle of the seventeenth century, an agitation in favor of greater freedom in the musical part of the Church service than was then tolerated. This brought on a controversy that extended over a century and ended in the establishment of volunteer choirs, psalm tune teachers, singing schools, musical conventions, secular singing societies, and the other forces that have co-operated to produce the high culture in music which Boston now enjoys. This polemical warfare, though felt, was far less influential in New York than in the cities of New England. While it was in progress the work of Anglicising New York was steadily going on, and Trinity Church was growing rapidly in wealth and influence, and preparing to take her place as the leader in musical culture. In wealth and respectability the Dutch Reformed Church was the only one that could cope with her, and the incubus of the Genevan Psalter prevented this from becoming a rival in promoting music. Trinity drew her musicians from England. It is likely that the first organ in the country stood within her walls, but a stronger proof than this of the early zeal of Trinity Church in respect to music is found in another fact recorded in Dr. Ritter's book (again, however, without citation of authority or adequate discussion): Handel's "Messiah" was performed in Trinity

Church, with organ accompaniment, as long ago as January 9, 1770, and repeated in each of the two succeeding years. This performance took place a little less than twenty-eight years after the original production of the work under Handel's direction in the New Music Hall, in Fishamble street, Dublin (April 13, 1742,); it was only eleven years after Handel's death (April 13, 1759,); it was more than fourteen years before the great Handel Commemoration in Westminster Abbey, on which occasion King George III, by a wave of his hand, commanded a repetition of the "Hallelujah" and "Amen" choruses (May 29, and June 5, 1784,); it was twenty years before Mozart wrote the additional accompaniments at the request of Baron von Sweten, for the performance of the oratorio in the hall of the *Hofbibliothek* in Vienna (March, 1789,); it was nearly forty-nine years earlier than the first performance of the oratorio by the Handel and Haydn Society of Boston (Christmas, 1818,), and eleven years before the custom of an annual performance of "The Messiah" in the Christmas-tide was introduced by the Cæcilian Society of London (1791).

It ought to be a matter of pride with the Protestant Episcopal Church, that the history of choral societies in New York traced back leads into its walls. The Handel and Haydn Society, of which Dr. Ritter records that it had "a brief but brilliant existence," grew out of a concert movement gotten up for the purpose of raising funds for re-building the Zion Church. Its successor was the Choral Society, to which is conceded the palm of excellence over all the vocal societies in existence at the beginning of the third decade of the present century. This society had its inception in a meeting held in September, 1823, in the Episcopal Charity School Room, and its studies were carried on in the lecture room of St. George's Church in Beekman street. It had a president and three vice-presidents, all of whom were clergymen. Something of the numerical strength and artistic taste of this early society is indicated by the preserved record of its first public concert. This took place on April 20, 1824, in St. George's Church, the forces employed being a choir of fifty voices and an orchestra of twenty instruments. It is significant of the extent of the Handel cult which had already been developed that ten of the fourteen numbers of the programme were compositions of that musical giant. The choir sang "Lift up your Heads," from "The Messiah," "To Thee, Cherubim" (from the "Dettingen Te Deum," probably), and "Sing unto the Lord," besides Mozart's motet, "O God, when Thou Appearest," and the "Hallelujah," from Beethoven's "Mount of Olives," the latter piece receiving, on this occasion, its first performance in New York, and being given with such good effect that it had to be repeated.

The Choral Society's dissolution, which came unaccountably early, left the musical field in the possession of The New York Sacred Music Society, which is the first in the list of those societies which were begotten in discord. It, too, was born in Zion Church, which seems to have been unusually active in the cultivation of choral music. This Church, as early as 1823, had a capable and numerous choir, that maintained an organized existence under the name of the Zion Church Musical Association. In the year mentioned the choristers of the Church applied to the vestry for an increase of salary or permission to give a concert. The vestry refused both requests. The choir presented a memorial maintaining the justice of the choristers' demand. The vestry, in formal action, characterized this as an interference with their rights and duties. The choir withdrew from the church, but having become attached to the cultivation of sacred music, a portion of the choir organized a society to continue that cultivation and called it The New York Sacred Music Society. The first concert of this Society took place a month earlier than that of the Choral Society. It was given in the Presbyterian Church in Provost street, and the choral numbers consisted of English anthems and an English version of the Marseillaise Hymn. Gradually, with growth in numbers, the order of music practiced by the Society was bettered, until, on the programme of a concert given on February 28, 1827, for the benefit of the Greek fund, we find, besides the Marseillaise Hymn (whose inspiriting air seems to

have made it popular with a people whose patriotism
still felt the influence of the grand passions created by
the early struggles of the Republic), the "Hallelujah"
of Handel as well as of Beethoven. The choir now
numbered sixty voices, and in this concert Malibran
sang "Angels Ever Bright and Fair." A pretty episode connected with her singing is related by a writer
in a musical journal of the time. Says the reporter:

During the performance of the song, so silent was the
audience that not even a whisper was to be heard. She
performed it beautifully, as a matter of course, although
the admirers of the simplicity of Handel had to regret
the introduction of so much ornament. She was "clad in
robes of virgin white," and at the words "Take, O, take
me to your care," she raised her hands and eyes in an
imploring attitude to heaven in so dramatic and touching a
manner as to electrify the audience, and to call down a
universal outburst of approbation—a very unusual occurrence
in a church of this country.

In 1831 The Sacred Music Society began a movement that entitles it to be called the real first pre-
cursor of the Oratorio Society. It then began the
study of an entire oratorio. There had long been talk
of oratorios, but the word was then used in the sense of
a concert made up of miscellaneous pieces of sacred
music. The loftier ambition which now fired the Society seems to have been inspired by the director then
recently engaged. This was U. C. Hill, a musician of
restless energy, to whom this country is indebted for
the organization of the New York Philharmonic Society.

The oratorio chosen was naturally, if not inevitably, "The Messiah." The work was studied so assiduously that by November of the same year the Sacred Music Society was ready to perform it. The concert took place in St. Paul's Chapel on November 18, and the forces employed numbered seventy-four voices and a band of thirty-eight instruments. The Chapel was filled with listeners, the receipts amounted to $900, and the oratorio was repeated twice within the next two months. Since then Handel's "Messiah" has been the starting-point of all our singing societies, and the Oratorio Society, in reverently preserving this tradition in its annual performance of the oratorio in the Christmas-tide, is paying a just tribute to the master and the work which have been more powerful in their influence than all else in the furthering of choral music. Fortunately for the cause, the custom is a profitable one, since the annual performance always draws a crowded house, and thus furnishes money which makes the bringing out of new works possible.

The Sacred Music Society, encouraged by the success which attended this first complete performance of an oratorio in New York City, added Haydn's "Te Deum" and "Creation" to its repertory, and produced oratorios annually thereafter until 1849, when it was succeeded by the New York Harmonic Society. For a short time it had a rival in the Academy of Sacred Music, started in 1832 by T. Hastings, who developed it out of meetings of church choirs, but the opposition never grew strong. An instance of the enterprising spirit of The Sacred Music Society was the production of Mendelssohn's "St. Paul" within two years after its first performance at Düsseldorf.

The succeeding period in the history of choral societies in New York carries it down to a time within the memory of most of the persons actively interested in them to-day, and is thus summarized in Dr. Ritter's book : *

About 1844 a new musical society was formed in New York—The Musical Institute. In September, 1846, Haydn's "Seasons," and afterwards other oratorios, were produced. On April 11, 1848, Schumann's secular cantata, "Paradise and the Peri," was brought out by this organization. Mr. Timm was the conductor. The chorus numbered about one hundred and twenty voices, with an orchestra of sixty musicians. Schumann was very much pleased when he heard of this performance in New York. Mr. Timm also brought Rossini's "Stabat Mater" out for the first time in America.

The Musical Institute, also, was short-lived. Towards 1850 musical affairs regarding societies in New York must have offered a discouraging aspect. All the older organizations were in a most demoralized state. On September 17, 1849, a meeting was held at the Coliseum Rooms of the great body of professors and amateurs of music, to form a plan for uniting the vocal strength of the inert societies of New York, to-wit: The Vocal Society, The Sacred Music Society, and The American Musical Institute. "We hope," says the circular, "there will be a full

---

* "Music in America," page 277.

meeting, and that means may be devised to form an union upon a broad and liberal footing. If so desired an object can be accomplished, New York will have a vocal society hardly to be surpassed in Europe, and not to be approached by any city in the Union." On Monday, September 24, the proposed meeting took place. The new society was ushered into the musical world under the name of the New York Harmonic Society. A constitution (this was invariably looked upon as a very important instrument; but it never prevented a society from becoming careless of its artistic duties, or going prematurely to pieces) was adopted, and a fund of five thousand dollars was to be formed. The prospects of the new society were in every respect bright. Rehearsals were at once begun, at first under the voluntary direction of Mr. H. C. Timm. The first oratorio to be given was "The Messiah." Mr. Th. Eisfeld was elected as the permanent conductor.

On the evening of May 10, 1850, the New York Harmonic Society gave its first public performance. The work of the society seems to have been, on the whole, satisfactory to its friends and supporters. On November 9, the same year, "The Messiah" was repeated, with no less a singer than Jenny Lind as the soprano soloist. On June 28, 1851, Mendelssohn's "Elijah" was performed at Tripler Hall. * * * The next oratorio given was Haydn's "Seasons."

In 1863 a rival society was formed out of a number of dissatisfied members, under the name of The Mendelssohn Society. The old story. It was thought a better plan, when any one society found it difficult to do efficient work, to have two, in order to give the public a double dose of inefficient work. But, having two societies, more men could be appointed to serve on music committees, and two positions were created for conductors, and each one had the chance of being considered the greater of the two. * * * The conductors of the Har-

monic Society were H. C. Timm, Th. Eisfeld, G. F. Bristow, C. Bergman, G. W. Morgan, F. L. Ritter, and, after
the resignation of the last gentleman, J. Peck, in whose
hands it softly went to sleep. The Society experienced,
in the course of its career, numerous re-organizations, but
none of them could save it from final dissolution. Its
rival society, The Mendelssohn Society, lived a similar
existence and died a similar death. Bristow, Morgan,
Berge, Thomas, Singer, alternately acted as conductors of
this latter society.

A few small errors have crept into this hasty out-
line of a long period of choral activity, which hardly
does justice to some of the work of the two societies
mentioned. Otto Singer was at no time director of
the Mendelssohn Society, but its pianist, under the directorship of Mr. Thomas. The old members of the
organization are anxious, too, that their establishment
of the new society shall not be looked upon in the
light of an ordinary defection from the Harmonic Society, but as an original movement to create a choir
with higher aims than were held at the time by the
older organization. The Mendelssohn Society had some
proud moments in its career, but most of them seem
to have grouped themselves around another attraction
than simple choral excellence. Thus it reached the
pinnacle of its greatness when it made its yearly series
of concerts the medium through which Christine Nilsson first became known to the American public. In
this it followed in the footsteps of its great rival,
which was periodically galvanized into active life by

the coming of Mme. Parepa to sing in the annual performance of "The Messiah."

A more significant fact in connection with the Mendelssohn Society, as showing how unstable was its frame, was the episode which caused its dissolution. The appearance of Mlle. Nilsson at its concerts brought the society into business relations with Mr. Strakosch, then the fair singer's manager. Mr. Strakosch conceived the idea of producing Rossini's "Messe Solennelle," which was then a novelty, and wished to do so in connection with the Mendelssohn Society. The scheme of study suggested by Mr. Strakosch, however, called for meetings on Sundays. One portion of the Society protested, the other insisted, and the concern fell to pieces.

Among the most ambitious of the latter-day choral enterprises was The Church Music Association. This choir filled an important place, for a series of years, in the public eye, but such was its peculiar character, that its appeal to the public ear, and its influence upon choral culture, was out of all proportion small compared with the pomp and circumstance associated with it. It was a child of aristocracy, an abnormal development of a species of amateur organization which is not without its commendable virtues when kept within its natural limits. In the winter of 1868-'69 (I follow notes kindly furnished by one of the active spirits of The Church Music Association), Mr. George

T. Strong invited a double quartet of ladies and gentlemen to meet at his house, No. 113 Gramercy Park, to study the masses of Haydn and Mozart. At the same time he engaged the services of James Pech, Mus. Doc. Oxon., then organist of St. John's Chapel, in Varick street, to drill the singers and direct the performances which, with a small orchestra of strings to supplement the pianoforte accompaniment, were held in Mr. Strong's parlors. These chamber concerts of mass music proved to be so pleasant and interesting that several gentlemen who were admitted to them suggested that the scope of the enterprise be enlarged, by transferring the meetings to a hall, increasing the choir, and engaging a full orchestra for the accompaniments. The suggestion was received with favor, and at a meeting held formally to consider the plan several thousands of dollars were subscribed by enthusiastic supporters of the scheme, an organization was effected and officers were elected. These officers were George T. Strong, president; the Rev. W. H. Cooke, secretary; Charles E. Strong, treasurer; R. M. Tucker, E. H. Schermerhorn, and James Pech, executive committee. There was, besides these officers, a committee of twelve ladies of prominent positions in society who gave the Association at the outset a marked social status.

Thus was launched The Church Music Association. The principles upon which it was based were exceptional: all expenses were provided for by the individual subscriptions of a few gentlemen who received, pro rata, the number of tickets to which their subscriptions entitled them. No tickets were sold and the public was practically excluded from all participation in the enterprise. The management was exclusive, and the whole interests of the Association depended upon the caprice of a few gentlemen who were interested in the style of music cultivated. It is, therefore, not strange that its career was brief. During the five years of its existence it performed some good works in a creditable manner, though it would have been difficult, finally, to tell from the programmes alone how the managers justified themselves in the belief that they were carrying out the original purposes expressed in the name and professions of the Association. It fell early into the absurdity of singing scenes from operas, though there has never been a time within the last fifty years when this branch of the art has not been amply cultivated by lyric dramatic companies. Such prestige as comes from social patronage The Church Music Association, for a time at least, had in plenty, and it undoubtedly had the most exclusive and remarkable audiences ever gathered in New York to listen to concerts of its character. It was found necessary to change the conductor, and Mr. Charles E. Horsley, an English musician of fair fame, who had made a certain mark with his compositions, became the successor of Dr. Pech. But the seeds of dissolution had been sowed in the inception of the enterprise. A large number of the choristers were more interested in the social than in the artistic aspect of the Association, and as the novelty of the affair wore off, the interest of singers and supporters soon began to flag, and it fell to pieces by reason of its unstable foundation. It had started with no less than one hundred gentlemen pledged to a contribution of $100 for the first season. Of these men perhaps a dozen were actively and earnestly interested in music; the rest gave their money because solicited, and drew their reward from the pleasure afforded their wives and daughters. When the interest began to die out, such giving became perfunctory and finally ceased. In the last year of the choir it actually rested upon the liberality of two or three gentlemen only; the public was not concerned, and it died of too much aristocracy, leaving a record that speaks warningly to all friends of choral music, even while it gives testimony of the enthusiasm and earnestness of purpose which actuated its leading spirits. One of these, the Rev. W. H. Cooke, promptly transferred his interest to the Oratorio Society, of which he has been the president since 1876.

IV.

WE have now reached the period which saw the birth of the Oratorio Society. It was eleven years ago. The only society that was keeping up even the semblance of an active existence was The Church Music Association, which, as has been indicated, had no artistic *raison d'être*. The Harmonic Society, not yet out of existence, had fallen into a sad somnolency, from which it was aroused once a year in order that it might scramble through a performance of "The Messiah" at Christmas. The situation was one which could give only sorrow to genuine lovers of chorus singing. There were such in the city, but the experiences of a decade back had been of a kind that did not encourage further attempts at re-organization or original construction. So far as musical leaders were concerned the number of singers in the city was sufficiently large to enable them, when it was desired to introduce a choral work into a concert scheme, to get together a choir. The nature of the German societies, in which the social element, beautiful and praiseworthy in itself, was cultivated more assiduously than the musical, prevented them from becoming the energetic public cultivators of choral music which were needed. In their way they were as exclusive as The Church Music Association.

55

To make a new venture, and give it the foundation that would assure success and permanency, was a formidable thing, and challenged a careful study of the lessons of the past. Those lessons were chiefly warnings. How not to do it any thinking man familiar with music and musical people might have learned had he had the story of which I have given the outlines before him. But an equally important question was how to do it; and this called for a co-operation of elements which might fairly have been described at that time as novel. Let us glance at these elements; we can draw most of them from the story of the Berlin *Singakademie.*

First, singers with a real love for music, and a devotion to their work so great that they are willing to put their hearts into it; that being the case, the putting of their bodies into it becomes a pleasure, not a task.

Second, a director actuated by a burning zeal for his art, and not by mercenary considerations; a man of broad sympathies and liberal tastes; one who can win the affectionate regard of his singers, while commanding their respectful obedience. To do this high aims must be associated with thorough knowledge and that magnetic quality which is possessed by leaders of men. He must be such a teacher that study under him becomes exhilarating intellectual and emotional exercise, instead, as is the rule, wearying, soul - killing drudgery. Such a man has ideas outside of the printed page; he catches the spark from the inspiration which erstwhile moved the composer, and he communicates the thrill to those whom he instructs. In the hands of such a man no really great composition is dry or dead; Palestrina and Bach pulsate with life, as well as the passionate writers of this later day.

Third, a wise, discreet, confidence-inspiring, and confidence-possessing business administration. Here must be, ultimately, the strong props that give the society permanency. Here there must be the inspiriting influence of a love for art equal to that of the singers and the conductor, yoked with a willingness to bear a burden greater than that of either of the other factors. Here must lodge a sense of discipline, business ability, a willingness to make sacrifices of self, and a wisdom great enough to perceive the inevitability of annoyance and to discover the remedy, coupled with a spirit that can thrust itself between chafing elements, and take off the friction upon itself. This is the department that is confronted always with the problem—which singers and conductor are bound to forget, at least in the moments of study and performance—How shall the money be secured to supply the organism with the necessities of its existence? Vexing questions hamper the establishment of such an administration. Shall it be representative? Nothing else will be tolerated in the republic of music inside a political republic. But shall its actions be hampered and restricted at will by those who do not bear its burdens? Assuredly not. There must be a division of labors, a division of powers, a division of responsibilities, and the extent of each activity must be proportionate. The *Singakademie* is now ninety-three years old, but a flourishing, active, ever-young organization. It was founded in great wisdom, in deep devotion, in perfect love. Its musical affairs from the first were the portion of Fasch; its business affairs rested with the Board of Administration.

The Oratorio Society is not unique in that the immediate impulse toward its creation came from a woman, but the circumstance is one which ought to be gratifying to the fair singers in its ranks. One of the hopes cherished by Dr. Damrosch when he came to New York in 1871 on the invitation of the Arion, was that of mustering under his baton organizations similar to those which he had directed for fourteen years in Breslau, Germany. He had turned his thoughts toward a mixed choir, but his inquiries were all met with discouraging replies. He had therefore continued to work in the narrow and uncongenial field of the *Männerchor* all the time for the instrument which would enable him to move more forcefully and effectively in the duty that a conscientious musician always feels, of promoting the cultivation of music in the community in which he lives. In the Spring of 1873 the desire to found a singing society was quickened to new activity by a visit from a lady who had come to suggest the same need which he had already felt so keenly. The lady, having herself recently come from Cologne, where she had learned to love choral singing by practicing it much under the direction of Ferdinand Hiller, felt the absence of a singing society worthy of the name as a deprivation. She asked Dr. Damrosch if a new start ought not to be made. He told her his misgivings inspired by the discoveries he had made concerning the state of choral culture, but willingly offered to make an attempt in the direction suggested.

A plan of operations was agreed on. Dr. Damrosch sent invitations to a number of friends and supporters. These steps resulted in the holding of a meeting two weeks later at the house of Dr. Damrosch, in Thirty-fifth street, at which twelve or fifteen persons were present. The prospects of the proposed society were canvassed; there was a good deal of earnestness in the party, and it was determined to go on with the experiment. After each person had agreed to play the part of a missionary, and try to bring at least one voice, in addition to his or her own, to a rehearsal next week, the meeting adjourned. It had been the purpose at first to meet for practice in a private house, but as hopes grew sanguine, some one proposed trying to get the use of Trinity Chapel. Dr. Dix was seen, and the great Trinity corporation, true to its early traditions, gave the use of Trinity Chapel for the first meeting of the new choir.

The first meeting was therefore held in Trinity Chapel, and fifteen or eighteen persons participated in it. The work was begun earnestly and hopefully, Dr. Damrosch, like his illustrious predecessor in Berlin, giving his services as conductor gratuitously, and playing his own accompaniment. The zeal and intelligent energy of the director were admirably supplemented by the zeal and talents of some of the individual singers in the small choir, particularly Mr. Theodore Toedt, who has since developed into one of the most popular solo singers of the country, and Mrs. Damrosch, who was once a professional singer, and has done great service in leading the soprano choir ever since. Four or five meetings were held in Trinity Chapel, and then the customary summer vacation interrupted the study. In the fall, when it was hoped to renew the meetings, the zealous choristers were made to learn that all musical things were not necessarily harmonious in their relations with each other. Circumstances combined to deprive the Society of the further use of Trinity Chapel. The choir had grown too large to think of studying in a private house, and was in the unfortunate position of having neither funds nor home. An appeal was made to the pianoforte manufacturers. Mr. Knabe offered the free use of his wareroom in Fifth avenue, and the offer was thankfully accepted.

Under these circumstances study was resumed. But now the financial question came in and made its abiding place with the choir. It has ever been a stubborn guest, one that will not depart with the asking. It is true Mr. Knabe asked no reward for the use of his premises, but the meeting of the choir made it necessary that the pianos be moved to the sides of the room, and this entailed the first outlay upon the singers. On the first evening the gentlemen present assessed themselves to meet this expenditure and others which were imminent, such as for the purchase of music.

At the first informal meeting a committee had been appointed to draft a plan of organization and suggest a name for the society. The name agreed on was the one still borne, and the first officers were the following: president, Professor F. A. P. Barnard, president of Columbia College; treasurer, Morris Reno; secretary, Dr. Julius Sachs; musical director, Dr. Damrosch. Ferdinand von Inten did the Society good service as volunteer accompanist for some time after the meetings were removed to Knabe's warerooms. It will be seen that Mr. Reno shouldered the financial burden at the outset, and he has not yet put it down.

The growth of the choir, very gradual but steady, brought it to pass that the room put at the disposition of the Society by Mr. Knabe was too small. Thereupon Mr. Knabe gave the use of a larger room on the upper floor of his building. This was a long and narrow room, not well adapted to the uses of a singing society, but the choristers were fain to accept it. They were already feeling the drawback that has checked choral culture in this city for half a century—the need of a hall fitted for choir meetings. The weekly meetings were held at Knabe's, from October, 1873, to April, 1874. There, too, on December 3, 1873, the first concert of the young organization was given. It took place in the smaller room. An admission fee was not asked, but members were permitted to invite a number of friends. The interesting character of the entertainment can be read in the programme, which was as follows:

1. { *a*, CHORALE, " *To God in Whom I trust*," . . . Bach.
  { *b*, "AVE VERUM," . . . . Mozart.

2. TRIO, Op. 1, No. 2, ... Beethoven.
  MR. F. VON INTEN, DR. DAMROSCH, AND MR. F. BERGNER.

3. AIR, " *Shepherd, what art thou pursuing?* " (Acis and
  Galatea), ... Handel.
  MR. J. GRAF.

4. { *a*, "Adoramus Te," . . . . Palestrina.
  { *b*, " *O hills, O vales of pleasure!* " . . . . Mendelssohn.

5. AIR, " *With Verdure Clad*, ... Haydn.
  MISS L. MENDES.

6. { *a*, AIR on G string, ... Bach.
  { *b*, NOTTURNO, Op. 27, No. 2, ... Chopin.
  (Arranged for violin by Wilhelmj.)
  DR. DAMROSCH.

7. AIRS AND CHORUSES from " *Samson*," . . . Handel.
  MISS E. FORSTER, MR. GRAF, AND SOCIETY.

The impression made upon the friends of the singers by this concert was one of delight, and the effect reacted in the encouragement of the energetic band. One thing the programme told with clear emphasis— the high aim and ideal purpose of the conductor. It had not been customary, even with the societies that boasted high-sounding names, to sing the compositions of Palestrina and Bach. In the programmes of The Church Music Association there were records of some too ambitious attempts, but the burden of its concerts was given more to Vincent Wallace than to Bach. It is a commentary upon the attention which the newspaper press of the city gave to music at that time that a concert of such excellence of matter was noticed by but one journal. This was *The Tribune,* whose criticism, written by Mr. J. R. G. Hassard, had so much intelligent appreciation of the effort of the Society in it that I quote it:

The first concert of the New York Oratorio Society was given last night at Knabe's piano rooms, in Fifth avenue. The audience was a good one, the performance was creditable, and the Society may be said to have begun its public career under very favorable auspices. It has been but a few months in existence, and numbers, as yet, not more than fifty or sixty members, largely recruited, we should judge, from German families of the highest class—a section of the community which manifests a better taste and warmer enthusiasm for music, and much more perseverance in the drudgery that vocal societies must undergo, than any other nationality. In the person of Dr. Leopold Damrosch, the Society has secured a valuable conductor—a man of culture, sound scholarship, energy, and personal magnetism; and the result of good training was consequently conspicuous last night. Of course we do not look for perfection in a new chorus; but we found many merits in the first performance of the Oratorio Society which are painfully missed in the concerts of older organizations. These ladies and gentlemen sang with correct intonation, firm attack, and a great deal of expression; and if they continue in the road upon which they have entered with so much promise, they will do some capital work before many seasons have passed. Their programme last night was not too ambitious. Besides a few unhackneyed selections from Handel, and Mendelssohn's beautiful and well-known "Farewell to the Forest," it contained a choral of J. S. Bach's, Mozart's "Ave Verum," and a noble "Adoramus Te" of Palestrina's, which we wish all our modern church organists could have been taken in a body to hear. Solemnity and devotion were in every line of it, and the Society sang it beautifully. Dr. Damrosch takes the *tempi* of most of the choruses with more freedom than has been customary in New York, varying the accent and expression by that means with rather striking effect; and although he must be, on that account, rather a difficult conductor to follow, the Society seems to have a perfect understanding with him.

The influence of this concert, as has been indicated, was to stimulate the enlistment of members. The public learned that a choral organization worthy of the name had again entered the field. Singers who were weary of the old *régime*, found a spirit in harmony with theirs in the new Society. Meanwhile study was prosecuted with unabated zeal, and by February,

1874, the Oratorio Society was ready to give its second concert. There was no lack of willingness to work on the part of those concerned in the government of the Society, but a sad lack of knowledge concerning the business management of its concerts. This was comically illustrated on the occasion of the second concert. The wisdom which had marked the first steps of the undertaking, dictated also that the Society, to become a real factor in the sum of the musical culture of the City, must come in contact with the public. But the efforts made to this end were timid. It was felt that another concert within the narrow confines of Mr. Knabe's room would not do. So Association Hall was rented for the concert, while the rehearsals still took place in the long, narrow room above the salesroom in the piano house. There was no public advertisement of the proposed entertainment, and the effort to enlist public interest and public support was restricted to personal solicitations by the members of the Society among their friends. On the night of the concert Mr. Reno learned, to his considerable surprise, from the janitor of the hall, that there were persons waiting at the door to buy tickets of admission. He had never suspected the need of opening the box-office before, but now he promptly installed the janitor there, and the result was an unexpected addition of $20 or $25 to the Society's funds.

The character of the second concert, as will be seen from the programme (printed in the Appendix), was similar to the first. There was the same maintenance of a high ideal, and the same judicious wisdom displayed regarding the popular desire for variety. On the programme was printed the following statement touching the aims and hopes of the Society:

In presenting the programme of this *soirée* to the public, the artistic management of the Society would presume to refer briefly to the objects pursued by the organization. The cultivation of the highest style of sacred and secular music has been designated in its prospectus as its aim; and though the study and public recitals of oratorios is one of the duties that the Society has assumed, its field of operations is considerably more extended. A vast literature of classical church music, and of universally admired secular compositions, might be named, of which but a small part has hitherto been studied and appreciated in this country; works of such transcendent beauty and excellence deserve to be revealed to our audiences.

It was encouraging to the Society to observe the appreciation which one of Palestrina's smaller compositions, hitherto unknown in this city, met with at the first *soiree*; of this composer, as also of such great masters as Lotti, Anerio, Gabrieli, Orlando di Lasso, Bach, Handel, Purcell, and very many others, there exist numerous equally celebrated compositions. The programmes of the previous and present *soirée* serve to indicate how the Society has endeavored to carry out its objects in this its first season. The encouragement received from the public at large, as well as the steady accession of new members to the chorus, permit us to look forward to a worthy close of the present season by the production of an entire oratorio.

The hope expressed in the last line of this address was realized in the performance at the third concert, which took place on May 12, 1874, in Steinway Hall, of Handel's "Samson," with full orchestral accompaniment. The Society still numbered less than a hundred members, but the testimony of the critics told of the whole-hearted style of their singing and the certainty of their attack, which resulted in the emission of that healthy and robust volume of sound which has been characteristic of the Society's performances ever since. "Samson" was the last work studied in the quarters provided by the public-spirited generosity of Mr. Knabe. With its production the Oratorio Society entered upon what it has since followed as its mission, and though a year or two elapsed before it reached its full stature as a choral organization, and had within its own ranks the numbers which are required to give adequate expression to the massive effects of the great choral writers, it was able, on Christmas evening of 1874, to accept the beautiful duty of performing "The Messiah" from the palsied hands of the Harmonic Society —a duty which it has fulfilled every year since. That there should be no want of effectiveness in the first performance of the work, it invited the co-operation of the Handel and Haydn Society of Brooklyn, of which Dr. Damrosch had been elected director. In turn the Oratorio Society assisted in the performance in Brooklyn. This reciprocity was practised for some time, with mutual benefit, but had finally to be abandoned because of the difficulty of moving the large choirs.

A difficulty from which the Oratorio Society is yet suffering now confronted the Board of Directors. Study in Mr. Knabe's upper floor room became practically impossible, and other quarters had to be found. No hall in the city had been arranged to accommodate the study of singing societies. The lecture rooms of churches were, on the whole, most practicable in the distribution of the furniture, but even they were far from perfect, in addition to being extremely difficult to get. Time and again has this lack in New York been deplored; time and again have public-spirited men in one or the other musical organization discussed the feasibility of undertaking the task of building a hall suitable for high-class choral and symphonic concerts, and as often have they been frightened back by the humiliating reflection that, while it is impossible for one organization to do the work, the want of harmony between the various organizations puts a seemingly insurmountable obstacle in the way of co-operation. Hence, concerts continue to be given in the Academy of Music, and rehearsals take place here and there in ill-fitted halls.

Within the eleven years of the existence of the Oratorio Society it has occupied eight study-rooms. From Knabe's it went to the reading room of the Young Men's Christian Association, where it was housed during the season of 1874–75; from 1875 to 1877 it made use

of the chapel of Dr. Crosby's Church; thence it removed to a room over the German Savings Bank. All
these places had to be hired, and the burden was
heavily felt by the young organization. During the
study months of the seasons of 1878–79 and 1879–80
it was again the grateful guest of Trinity Corporation,
the Rev. Henry C. Potter, D. D., now Assistant Bishop
of the diocese of New York, always a warm friend of
music, and especially of choral music (at present he
is a director of the Oratorio Society), having secured
for its use gratuitously, first, Grace Chapel, in Twenty-
third street, and afterward Grace Chapel, in Fourteenth
street. At the beginning of the season of 1881–82 it
was found necessary, on account of increased member-
ship, to change the rehearsal room, and now the large
hall in the building of the Young Men's Christian Association, the so-called Association Hall, was hired; this
is yet the study-room of the choir. From 1874 till 1882
the concerts of the Oratorio Society were given in
Steinway Hall; since the latter date they have been
given in the Academy of Music.

It is hardly necessary to follow all the footsteps of
the Society from the time it set out upon its course
fully equipped till now; it is sufficient to show how its
steady growth was accentuated at intervals by achievements of particular magnitude. Beginning with "Samson," one after another of the great works in the Oratorio class was performed with adequate forces and

fine spirit; of Handel's, "Judas Maccabeus," "The
Messiah," "Alexander's Feast," "L'Allegro, Il Pensi-
eroso ed Il Moderato," reaching the pinnacle in this
department in "Israel in Egypt," in 1882; of Haydn's,
"The Creation" and "The Seasons;" of Mendelssohn's, "St. Paul" and "Elijah;" of Bach's, the
Church cantatas, "God's Time is the Best Time" and
"Vain and Fleeting," and his gigantic master-work,
"The Passion, according to St. Matthew." In addition to this diligent cultivation of the classic writers,
the Society has placed to its credit commendable enterprise in the work of acquainting the public with
some of the most monumental of the latter-day compositions. Brahms's "A German Requiem" owed its
introduction in English to this spirit, and Berlioz's colossal "Messe des Mortes" received its first performance in this country at the hands of the Oratorio Society. Nothing can show plainer how wide-spread its
activity has been than an enumeration of the works
which it has performed, and this is given herewith in
tabular form. It should be premised, however, with
the statement, that it does not represent the sum of
the Oratorio Society's accomplishments, but enumerates
only those works which were sung in the regular concerts of the Society. As will be seen hereafter, these
concerts do not round out the Society's work:

CHORAL WORKS PERFORMED IN THE CONCERTS
OF THE ORATORIO SOCIETY, 1873-1884.

First Performance.	Times Performed.	COMPOSER.	TITLE OF WORK.
1873	1	Bach	Chorale, "To God, in Whom I trust."
1874	1	Bach	Chorale, "Now to th' Eternal God."
1877	1	Bach	Cantata, "Actus Tragicus." [thew."
1880	2	Bach	"The Passion, according to St. Mat-
1882	1	Bach	Cantata, "Vain and Fleeting."
1879	1	Beethoven	March from "The Ruins of Athens."
1882	1	Berlioz	"Grande Messe des Mortes."
1877	1	Brahms	"A German Requiem."
1883	1	Cowen	"St. Ursula."
1875	1	Damrosch	"Ruth and Naomi."
1882	1	Damrosch	"Sulamith."
1877	1	Gluck	Selections from "Orpheus."
1874	1	Handel	"Samson." [Priest."
1874	1	Handel	Coronation Anthem, "Zadock the
1874	10	Handel	"The Messiah."
1877	1	Handel	"Judas Maccabeus."
1878	1	Handel	"Alexander's Feast," [erato."
1881	1	Handel	"L'Allegro, Il Pensieroso ed Il Mod-
1882	1	Handel	"Israel in Egypt."
1874	1	M. Haydn	"Tenebræ factæ sunt."
1877	2	Haydn	"The Creation."
1878	2	Haydn	"The Seasons."
1879	1	Kiel	"Christus" (two parts).
1876	1	Liszt	"Christus" (first part). [Pleasure!"
1873	1	Mendelssohn	Part-song, "O Hills, O Vales of
1874	1	Mendelssohn	Motet, "Laudate pueri Dominum."
1875	2	Mendelssohn	"St. Paul."
1876	2	Mendelssohn	"First Walpurgis Night."
1876	4	Mendelssohn	"Elijah."
1878	1	Mendelssohn	"Psalm CXIV."
1873	1	Mozart	"Ave Verum."
1873	1	Palestrina	"Adoramus Te."
1882	1	Rubinstein	"Tower of Babel." [in E flat.
1875	1	Schubert	*Kyrie, Sanctus, and Agnus,* from Mass
1876	1	Schumann	"Paradise and the Peri."
1879	1	Wagner	Chorale from "Die Meistersinger."

The work which the Oratorio Society has done outside of its own concerts is well worthy of mention in
a review of its career.   We have seen that in the
early years of its existence it received assistance from
and gave assistance to the Handel and Haydn Society
of Brooklyn.   A similar reciprocal arrangement was
subsequently entered into with Theodore Thomas's Orchestra and the Philharmonic Society of Brooklyn.
Mr. Thomas provided the accompaniments to the performances of the Society during the seasons of 1875
and 1876, and the Society returned the compliment
by singing for Mr. Thomas the choral part of Beethoven's Ninth Symphony, which thus received a memorable performance.   Subsequently this lovely harmony
of action was disturbed by reason of the fact that the
Thomas Orchestra having been dissolved, the same energetic spirit that had piloted the young Society to success began an agitation which saved the City from
being dependent upon one conservative organization
for its orchestral music.   In 1877 Dr. Damrosch, in
company with a number of gentlemen actively interested in the cultivation of orchestral music, brought
about the establishment of the Symphony Society, whose
fortunes since then have been closely identified with
those of the Oratorio Society.   Though there is inde-
pendence of action on each side there is harmonious
co-operation in the respective concerts.   The beauty
and value of this co-operation received its brightest

illustration in the series of concerts under the auspices of the Symphony Society in 1879 and 1880, in which Berlioz's "La Damnation de Faust" was given with a brilliancy that created a popular *furore* such as the annals of music in New York till then had not revealed. The Ninth Symphony and Berlioz's "Romeo and Juliet" have also been given by the union, the former three times up to date. Concerts have also been given by the Society in Philadelphia and in Brooklyn.

The most significant outcome of the reciprocity existing between the Symphony and Oratorio Societies is, however, yet to be mentioned. As a member of the Board of Directors of the Symphony Society, Mr. Reno, early in 1880, suggested the holding of a great musical festival under the joint management of the two societies. The proposition was agreed to and the outcome was the festival of 1881, one of the most memorable in the history of music in the United States. The festival was held in the armory of the Seventh Regiment on May 3, 4, 5, 6, and 7, 1881. The chorus numbered 1,200, the nucleus of the body being the Oratorio Society, which formed Section A; Section B was an independent body in New York City; Section C was organized in Newark; Section D, in Brooklyn; Section E, in Jersey City; and Section F, in Nyack. The various sections began the study of the festival music in September, 1880, under their respective leaders—Dr. Damrosch, of Section A; Walter Damrosch, of Section B; Walter Damrosch and Henry Feigl, of Section C; Augustin Cortada, of Section D; Louis Jacoby, of Section E, and G. D. Wilson, of Section F. During September, October, November, December, of 1880, and January, of 1881, the sections continued their separate study, being visited at regular intervals by Dr. Damrosch; after the latter date these separate rehearsals were supplemented by mass rehearsals, under Dr. Damrosch, in the hall of Cooper Union. Besides this grand chorus an additional chorus of 1,200 young ladies from the Normal College and 250 boys from the church choirs of the city was organized to take part in the afternoon concerts. This was done by the conductor with the hope that through the impulse which would be given by the participation of these young people in a performance of the festival music, their interest in and appreciation of music of the highest order would be awakened and a powerful lever thus be applied for the promotion of musical culture in the future. The young ladies' choir was in charge of Professor George Mangold; the boys' choir was organized by Mr. John D. Prince. The orchestra numbered two hundred and fifty-one performers. It was selected most carefully by Dr. Damrosch, and contained all the leading musicians of New York (including the orchestras of both the Symphony and Philharmonic Societies), besides a number of excellent artists from

Boston, Cincinnati, Philadelphia, and Baltimore. The principal choral works performed were Handel's "Dettingen Te Deum," Rubinstein's "Tower of Babel," "The Messiah," Berlioz's "Grande Messe des Mortes," and Beethoven's Ninth Symphony. The artistic success of the festival was decided, and, despite the tremendous cost of the undertaking (the rent bill for the hall alone amounting to $10,000), the balance was in favor of the management when accounts were struck.

The causes of the success of the Oratorio Society are not far to seek; they consist in the realization, in a high degree, of the ideals set out in the opening sentences of this chapter. For five years after the founding of the Society, Dr. Damrosch's services were given to it without reward or recompense, and the record of work accomplished is as eloquent a certificate of his qualifications for the post of musical director as could be granted. Only those who have been amongst the singers during their practice hours know how whole-heartedly, intelligently, and sympathetically this musician throws himself into the work in hand. Aside from the fact that he possesses in a high degree those elements which I have enumerated heretofore as the outfit of an ideal choral conductor, Dr. Damrosch is a man of refined intellectual culture, one versed in the art of voice culture, and he has the happy faculty of quickening the minds as well as the hearts of his singers by his method of giving brief expositions of the contents of the compositions which he desires to teach them. In this manner he enlists the interest and affections as well of his singers in the composition, and inspires them to sing with the spirit and understanding, a work in which he is aided by the co-operation of his son Walter as accompanist. He never permits the difficulties of a piece of music to crush the spirit of his singers by their dull weight, but stimulates them by pointing out the goal that will be reached when the difficulties are overcome. By such means he keeps the mind of the Society elastic and makes the study of new works a recreation. The manner in which it is done, moreover, secures the element of success which is the primary one — earnest, enthusiastic, willing singers. The possession of these in large numbers is one of the best fruits which the Oratorio Society can show. There is, of necessity, a large transient element in every singing society, and there will be so long as American society continues in its present state of restlessness and fermentation. People come and go; remove from one end of the island to the other; take up homes in the suburban districts; change their habits of life; and all these things add to the difficulty of putting stability into a choir. Every year old and experienced singers are compelled to sing to them familiar music in order that new comers may learn, and their willingness to do this in the Oratorio Society is an evidence of their love for choral music and their admiration for their leader.

To the wisdom of the directors, is largely due the placing of the Society on a firm financial footing, and the development of a system of administration which insures stability and makes continued progress possible. The difficult task of always making both ends meet has been before them from the time when after the first modest rehearsal in Mr. Knabe's room the gentlemen present assessed themselves to pay the janitor for clearing the floor of pianofortes. One secret of the success of their administration has lain, without doubt, in the adherence to a purpose not to burden the singers with the financial embarrassments which inevitably come to musical organizations in their early years. We have seen from Dr. Ritter's words how discouraging financial failure is to singers. Such failures clung persistently to the heels of the Oratorio Society during its youthful years; but care was taken that they caused no apprehension in the ranks of the choristers. Whatever was the state of the treasury at the end of a season the treasurer's report showed a balance on the right side. Sometimes the requisite sum was raised by subscriptions among the directors; it always came, and the fruit of the self-sacrifice was the development of a system of management which, of late, has kept the Oratorio Society in easy financial circumstances, and enabled its musical director to pursue his aims in the production of works without fear of embarrassing the organization. Among those who have distinguished themselves by their devotion to the interests of the Society are Mr. Morris Reno, its treasurer, who attended from the beginning not only to the financial affairs, but also to the numerous details which the public performances require and which involve an endless amount of labor and sacrifice of time; Mr. S. M. Knevals, an active member and director for eight years; the Rev. W. H. Cooke, president since 1876, in deed as well as name, and Mr. W. B. Tuthill, for three years secretary, an energetic officer and a strict disciplinarian.

If, as Goethe says, it is the curse of a wicked deed that it must go on giving birth to new wickednesses, it is also the blessing of a virtuous act that many virtues follow in its train. The measure of merit due the Oratorio Society is not full when the record of its direct accomplishment is written — there remain the products of its influence. Mr. Thomas's Chorus Society can fairly be counted amongst its fruits, and it has either stimulated to new life, or caused the organization of a number of societies in Newark, Jersey City, Nyack, Rochester, and other places.

APPENDIX.

APPENDIX

APPENDIX.

OFFICERS OF THE ORATORIO SOCIETY.

SEASON OF 1873-1874.

President—F. A. P. BARNARD.

Treasurer—MORRIS RENO.

Secretary—DR. J. SACHS.

Musical Director—DR. LEOPOLD DAMROSCH.

Accompanist—AUGUST CORTADA.

1874-1875.

President—S. W. COE.

Treasurer—MORRIS RENO.

Secretary—S. V. SPEYER.

Musical Director—DR. LEOPOLD DAMROSCH.

Accompanist—AUGUST CORTADA.

1875-1876.

President—W. L. GOODWIN.

Treasurer—MORRIS RENO.

Secretary—R. M. MARTIN.

Musical Director—DR. LEOPOLD DAMROSCH.

———

Accompanist—AUGUST CORTADA.

1876-1877.

President—THE REV. W. H. COOKE.

Treasurer—MORRIS RENO.

Secretary—R. L. HARSELL.

Musical Director—DR. LEOPOLD DAMROSCH.

———

Accompanist—AUGUST CORTADA.

1877-1878.

President—THE REV. W. H. COOKE.

Treasurer—MORRIS RENO.

Secretary—R. L. HARSELL.

Musical Director—DR. LEOPOLD DAMROSCH.

———

Accompanist—WALTER DAMROSCH.

1878-1879.

President—THE REV. W. H. COOKE.

Treasurer—MORRIS RENO.

Secretary—R. L. HARSELL.

Musical Director—DR. LEOPOLD DAMROSCH.

———

Accompanist—WALTER DAMROSCH.

1879-1880.

President—THE REV. W. H. COOKE.

Treasurer—MORRIS RENO.

Secretary—A. L. TRAIN.

Musical Director—DR. LEOPOLD DAMROSCH.

———

Accompanist—WALTER DAMROSCH.

1880-1881.

President—THE REV. W. H. COOKE.

Treasurer—MORRIS RENO.

Secretary—A. L. TRAIN.

Musical Director—DR. LEOPOLD DAMROSCH.

———

Accompanist—WALTER DAMROSCH.

1881-1882.

President—THE REV. W. H. COOKE.

Treasurer—MORRIS RENO.

Secretary—WILLIAM B. TUTHILL.

Musical Director—DR. LEOPOLD DAMROSCH.

———

Accompanist—WALTER DAMROSCH.

1882-1883.

President—THE REV. W. H. COOKE.

Treasurer—MORRIS RENO.

Secretary—WILLIAM B. TUTHILL.

Musical Director—DR. LEOPOLD DAMROSCH.

———

Accompanist—WALTER DAMROSCH.

1883-1884.

President—THE REV. W. H. COOKE.

Treasurer—MORRIS RENO.

Secretary—WILLIAM B. TUTHILL.

Musical Director—DR. LEOPOLD DAMROSCH.

———

Accompanist—WALTER DAMROSCH.

PROGRAMMES OF THE REGULAR CONCERTS OF THE ORATORIO SOCIETY.

First Season.

First Concert, December 3, 1873.

CHORALE, "*To God, in Whom I Trust,*" . . . . . J. S. Bach.

MOTET, "*Ave Verum,*" . . . . Mozart.

TRIO, *G Major, Op.* 1, *No.* 2, ... Beethoven.
MR. F. VON INTEN, DR. L. DAMROSCH,
MR. FREDERICK BERGNER.

AIR, "*Shepherd, what art Thou pursuing?*" (Acis and
Galatea), ... Handel.
MR. J. GRAF.

"*Adoramus Te,*" . . . . Palestrina.

PART SONG, "*O Hills, O Vales of Pleasure!*" . . Mendelssohn.

AIR, "*With Verdure Clad*" (Creation) . . . . . . Haydn.
MISS L. MENDES.

{ AIR (*on G string*) . . . . Bach.
{ NOTTURNO (*Op.* 27, *No.* 2), ... Chopin.
(Arranged for the violin by Wilhelmj.)
DR. LEOPOLD DAMROSCH.

85

AIR AND CHORUS, "*Return, O God of Hosts!*" and
"*To Dust his Glory*" (Samson), ... Handel.

Contralto—MISS E. FORSTER.

AIR AND CHORUS, "*Great Dagon has subdued our
foe*" (Samson), ... Handel.

Tenor—MR. J. GRAF.

SECOND CONCERT, FEBRUARY 26, 1874.

CHORALE, "*Now to th' Eternal God!*" . . . . . . J. S. Bach.

MOTET, "*Laudate pueri Dominum,*" . . . . . Mendelssohn.

MISS SIMON, MISS STRASBURGER, MISS KARFUNKEL.

Organ—MR. S. P. WARREN.

ARIA DI CHIESA, ... Stradella.

MR. A. SOHST.

DUET, "*Caro più amabile*, (Giulio Cæsare), ... Handel

MISS SIMON AND MISS MUNIER.

ORGAN SOLOS, { *a, Canon, No. 4, from op.* 56, . . Schumann.
{ *b, Moderato,* . . . . Gade.

MR. S. P. WARREN.

"*And the Angel,*" . . . . Orlando di Lasso.

"*Tenebræ factæ sunt,*" . . . . Michael Haydn.

AIR, "*Have Mercy upon me,*" (St. Matthew Passion,) . . . Bach.

MISS KARFUNKEL; Violin—DR. L. DAMROSCH;

Organ—MR. S. P. WARREN.

QUARTETS, { *a, Prayer, "O God, Thy goodness,"* . . Beethoven.
{ *b, Christmas Song,* . . . . Liszt.

MISS COLETTI, MISS KARFUNKEL.

MR. GRAF and MR. SOHST.

CORONATION ANTHEM, "*Zadock, the Priest,*" . . . Handel.

Third Concert, May 12, 1874.

Handel's Oratorio,

SAMSON.

With full Chorus, Orchestra, and Organ.

Miss Anna Simon, ⎫ Sopranos.
Miss L. Mendes, ⎭

Miss Antonia Henne, Contralto.

Mr. George Simpson, Tenor.

Mr. F. Remmertz, ⎫ Basses.
Mr. A. Sohst, ⎭

Mr. S. P. Warren, Organist.

Second Season.

First Concert, December 25, 1874.

Handel's Sacred Oratorio,

THE MESSIAH.

Miss Abbie Whinnery, Soprano.

Miss Anna Drasdil, Contralto.

Mr. George Simpson, Tenor.

Mr. A. E. Stoddard, Bass.

Mr. S. P. Warren, Organist.

Second Concert, February 22, 1875.

"Kyrie," "Sanctus," and "Agnus Dei," (Mass in E
flat,) first time, ...Schubert.

CONTRALTO AIR (*Semele*), ... Handel.

SCRIPTURAL IDYL, *Ruth and Naomi,* for Soli,
Chorus, and Orchestra, first time, . . . Dr. L. Damrosch.

Miss Harriet E. Bedloe, Soprano.

Miss Anna Drasdil, Contralto.

Mr. Alexander Bischoff, Tenor.

Mr. Franz Remmertz, Bass.

Mr. S. P. Warren, Organist.

Third Season.

First Concert, November 9, 1875.

Mendelssohn's Oratorio,

ST. PAUL.

Mrs. Imogene Brown, Soprano.
Miss Anna Drasdil, Contralto.
Mr. Alexander Bischoff, Tenor.
Mr. A. E. Stoddard, Baritone.

Second Concert, December 27, 1875.

Handel's Sacred Oratorio,

THE MESSIAH.

Miss Emma C. Thursby, Soprano.
Miss Anna Drasdil, Contralto.
Mr. George Simpson, Tenor.
Mr. A. E. Stoddard, Bass.
Mr. S. P. Warren, Organist.

Third Concert, February 28, 1876.

CHRISTUS, (first part) . . . . Liszt.
(For the first time in America.)

AIR, "*Nasce al bosco*" (Ezio), ... Handel.

THE FIRST WALPURGIS NIGHT, ... Mendelssohn.

Miss Mary Werneke, Soprano.
Mr. Alexander Bischoff, Tenor.
Mr. A. E. Stoddard, Baritone.
Mr. S. P. Warren, Organist.

FOURTH CONCERT, APRIL 26, 1876.

SCHUMANN'S CANTATA,

PARADISE AND THE PERI.

MISS IDA HUBBELL,
MISS ANNETTA WENTZ. } Sopranos.

MISS ANTONIA HENNE, Mezzo Soprano.

MR. GEORGE SIMPSON, Tenor.

MR. FRANZ REMMERTZ, Bass.

Fourth Season.

First Concert, November 8, 1876.

Mendelssohn's Oratorio,

ELIJAH.

Miss Henrietta Corradi, Soprano.
Miss Anna Drasdil, Contralto.
Mr. William Castle, Tenor.
Mr. A. E. Stoddard, Baritone.

And the Following Members of the Oratorio Society:

Miss M. Heimburg, Miss H. Obendorfer,
Miss E. Urchs, Mr. Frank Smith,
Mr. G. P. Warner.

Second Concert, December 25, 1876.

Handel's Sacred Oratorio,

THE MESSIAH.

Mrs. Imogene Brown, Soprano.
Miss Anna Drasdil, Contralto.
Mr. George Simpson, Tenor.
Mr. John F. Winch, Bass.

Third Concert, March 15, 1877.

CANTATA (Actus Tragicus), ... J. S. Bach.
(First time in America.)

SELECTIONS FROM ORPHEUS, ... Gluck.

A GERMAN REQUIEM, ... Brahms.

(First time in America.)

MISS MARIE HEIMBURG, Soprano.

MISS ANNA DRASDIL, Contralto.

MR. HENRY BRANDEIS, Tenor.

MR. A. E. STODDARD, Baritone.

FOURTH CONCERT APRIL 14, 1877.

HAYDN'S ORATORIO,

THE CREATION.

MISS EMMA C. THURSBY, Soprano.

MR. GEORGE SIMPSON, Tenor.

MR. A. E. STODDARD, Baritone.

Fifth Season.

FIRST CONCERT, NOVEMBER 15, 1877.

HANDEL'S ORATORIO,

JUDAS MACCABEUS.

MRS. IMOGENE BROWN, Soprano.
MISS ANTONIA HENNE, Contralto.
MR. JOSEPH MAAS, Tenor.
MR. A. E. STODDARD, Baritone.

SECOND CONCERT, DECEMBER 29, 1877.

HANDEL'S SACRED ORATORIO,

THE MESSIAH.

MISS EMMA C. THURSBY, Soprano.
MISS ANNA DRASDIL, Contralto.
MR. GEORGE SIMPSON, Tenor.
MR. F. REMMERTZ, Bass.
MR. S. P. WARREN, Organist.

THIRD CONCERT, FEBRUARY 28, 1878.

HAYDN'S ORATORIO,

THE SEASONS.

MRS. IMOGENE BROWN, Soprano.
MR. GEORGE SIMPSON, Tenor.
MR. A. E. STODDARD, Baritone.

Fourth Concert, April 25, 1878.

Mendelssohn's Oratorio,

ELIJAH.

MME. EUGENIE PAPPENHEIM, } Sopranos.
MISS MARY E. TURNER.

MISS ADELAIDE PHILIPPS, Contralto.

MR. ALEXANDER BISCHOFF, Tenor.

MR. MYRON WHITNEY, } Basses.
MR. A. E. STODDARD.

And the Following Members of the Oratorio Society:

MISS HELEN OBENDORFER, MISS E. URCHS,
MR. FRANK SMITH, MR. LEO GOLDMARK.

Sixth Season.

First Concert, November 30, 1878.

HANDEL'S ALEXANDER'S FEAST.

MENDELSSOHN'S CXIV PSALM.

Miss Helen Ames, Soprano.
Mr. William Courtney, Tenor.
Mr. Franz Remmertz, Bass.
Orchestra of the Symphony Society.

Second Concert, December 28, 1878.

Handel's Sacred Oratorio,

THE MESSIAH.

Miss Minnie Hauk, Soprano.
Miss Anna Drasdil, Contralto.
Mr. George Simpson, Tenor.
Mr. A. E. Stoddard, Bass.
Mr. Samuel P. Warren, Organist.

Third Concert, February 19, 1879.

Mendelssohn's Oratorio,

ST. PAUL.

Mrs. Mary L. Swift, Soprano.
Miss Anna Drasdil, Contralto.
Mr. George Simpson, Tenor.
Mr. Myron W. Whitney, Bass.

Fourth Concert, April 17, 1879.

CHRISTUS, (Christ's entry into Jerusalem and
    Resurrection), ... Friedrich Kiel.

(First time in America.)

LARGO, for Violin Solo and Strings, ... Handel.
(Arranged by Dr. L. Damrosch.)

AVE VERUM, ... Mozart.

CHORALE, (Die Meistersinger), ... Wagner.

AIR, "*Oh, pardon me,*" . . . . Bach.

MARCH (The Ruins of Athens), ... Beethoven.

Miss Antonio Henne, Mezzo Soprano.
Mrs. Florence Rice-Knox, Contralto.
Mr. Jacob Graf, Tenor.
Mr. A. Stoddard, Bass.
Herr August Wilhelmj, Violinist.

Seventh Season.

First Concert, November 29, 1879.

MENDELSSOHN'S ORATORIO,

ELIJAH.

MRS. MARY L. SWIFT, ⎫
MISS AMY SHERWIN, ⎭ Sopranos.

MISS ANNA DRASDIL, Contralto.

MR. CHRISTIAN FRITSCH, Tenor.

MR. FRANZ REMMERTZ, Bass.

And the following members of the Oratorio Society:

MISS CLARA OBENDORFER, MR. FRANK SMITH,
and MR. LEO GOLDMARK.

Second Concert, December 27, 1879.

HANDEL'S SACRED ORATORIO,

THE MESSIAH.

MISS EMMA THURSBY, Soprano.

MISS ANNA DRASDIL, Contralto.

MR. GEORGE SIMPSON, Tenor.

MR. FRANZ REMMERTZ, Bass.

MR. S. P. WARREN, Organist.

Third Concert, February 7, 1880.

Haydn's Oratorio,

THE CREATION.

Miss Letitia L. Fritch, Soprano.
Mr. Jacob Graf, Tenor.
Mr. Myron W. Whitney, Bass.

Fourth Concert, March 18, 1880.

Johann Sebastian Bach's

THE PASSION OF OUR LORD,

(According to St. Matthew.)

Mrs. Anna Granger Dow, Soprano.
Miss Mathilde Philipps, Contralto.
Mr. William J. Winch, Tenor.
Mr. John F. Winch, Bass.
Mr. George E. Aiken, Bass.
Mr. George F. Le Jeune, Organist.
Mr. Walter Damrosch, Pianist.
Choir of Boys from Trinity Parish.

Eighth Season.

FIRST CONCERT, NOVEMBER 27, 1880.

MENDELSSOHN'S ORATORIO,

ELIJAH.

MRS. MARY L. SWIFT, Soprano.

MISS ANNA P. SANGER, Soprano.

MISS ANNA DRASDIL, Contralto.

MRS. LILLIE G. NICKOLDS, Contralto.

MR. GEORGE SIMPSON, Tenor.

MR. GEORGE HENSCHEL, Baritone.

MR. REINHOLD HERRMANN, Bass.

MR. WALTER DAMROSCH, Organist.

SECOND CONCERT, DECEMBER 29, 1880.

HANDEL'S SACRED ORATORIO,

THE MESSIAH.

MISS LILLIAN BAILEY, Soprano.

MISS ANNA DRASDIL, Contralto.

MR. THEODORE J. TOEDT, Tenor.

MR. GEORGE HENSCHEL, Baritone.

MR. WALTER DAMROSCH, Organist.

APPENDIX.

THIRD CONCERT, FEBRUARY 26, 1881.

HANDEL'S

L'ALLEGRO, IL PENSIEROSO ED IL MODERATO.

(First time in New York.)

MRS. JULIE ROSEWALD, Soprano.

MISS ABBIE WHINNERY, Soprano.

MISS EMILY WINANT, Contralto.

MR. THEODORE J. TOEDT, Tenor.

MR. GEORGE HENSCHEL, Baritone.

MR. WALTER DAMROSCH, Organist.

𝕴intb Season.

First Concert, November 26, 1881.

SANCTUS, from the Messe des Mortes, ... Berlioz.

THE TOWER OF BABEL, a Sacred Opera, . . . Rubinstein.

Sig. Italo Campanini, Tenor.

Mr. Franz Remmertz, Bass.

Mr. Walter Damrosch, Organist.

Second Concert, December 28, 1881.

Handel's Sacred Oratorio,

THE MESSIAH.

Miss Hattie L. Simms, Soprano.

Miss Anna Drasdil, Contralto.

Mr. A. L. King, Tenor.

Mr. Franz Remmertz, Bass.

Mr. Walter Damrosch, Organist.

Third Concert, February 25, 1882.

Handel's Oratorio,

ISRAEL IN EGYPT.

Miss Ida W. Hubbell, Soprano.

Miss Antonia Henne, Contralto.

Mr. Theodore J. Toedt, Tenor.

Mr. John F. Winch, Bass.

Mr. Franz Remmertz, Bass.

Mr. Walter Damrosch, Organist.

Fourth Concert, April 21, 1882.

CANTATA, "*Vain and Fleeting*," . . . . J. S. BACH.

SULAMITH, a Cantata for Soli, Chorus, and Orchestra, ... Dr. L. DAMROSCH.

(First Performance.)

MISS HATTIE L. SIMMS, Soprano.

MRS. BELLE COLE, Contralto.

Tenth Season.

First Concert, November 16, 1882.

PRELUDE (Parsifal), ... Wagner.

ORCHESTRA.

GRAND MESSE DES MORTES, ... Berlioz.

SIGNOR RAVELLI, Tenor.

SEXTET, by MRS. HELEN AMES, MISS CHRISTINE DOSSERT, SIGNOR RAVELLI, HENRY WORAM, E. COLETTI, AND MAX HEINRICH.

Second Concert, December 27, 1882.

HANDEL'S SACRED ORATORIO,

THE MESSIAH.

MISS HENRIETTA BEEBE,	MISS ANNA DRASDIL,
MR. A. D. WOODRUFF,	MR. JOHN F. WINCH.

MR. WALTER DAMROSCH, Organist.

Third Concert, March 7, 1883.

MENDELSSOHN'S ORATORIO,

ELIJAH.

MME. GABRIELLE BOËMA,	MRS. O. H. FELLOWS,
MISS EMILY WINANT,	MRS. F. J. KIRPAL,
MR. JULES JORDAN,	MR. H. BERSIN,
MR. E. COLETTI,	MR. MAX HEINRICH.

Fourth Concert, April 19, 1883.

THE CREATION, ... Haydn.

JUBILATE AMEN, ... Bruch.

Miss Emma Juch,

Mr. A. D. Woodruff,   Mr. Max Heinrich.

Eleventh Season.

FIRST CONCERT, NOVEMBER 22, 1883.

CANTATA (St. Ursula), ...F. H. Cowen.

CANTATA (The First Walpurgis Night), . . . Mendelssohn.

MRS. E. ALINE OSGOOD, Soprano.

MISS HOPE GLENN, Contralto.

MR. THEODORE TOEDT, Tenor.

MR. A. E. STODDARD, Bass.

SECOND CONCERT, DECEMBER 27, 1883.

HANDEL'S

MESSIAH.

MRS. E. J. GRANT, Soprano.

MME. TREBELLI, Contralto.

MR. C. H. THOMPSON, Tenor.

MR. MAX HEINRICH, Bass.

MR. WALTER DAMROSCH, Organist.

Third Concert, March 13, 1884.

Johann Sebastian Bach's

THE PASSION OF OUR LORD,

(According to St. Matthew.)

Mrs. Emma A. Danforth, Soprano.

Mrs. Sarah B. Anderson, Contralto.

Mr. W. H. Stanley, Tenor.

Mr. Max Heinrich, Baritone.

Mr. C. E. Martin, Bass.

Mr. Walter Damrosch, Organist.

Fourth Concert, May 10, 1884.

Haydn's Oratorio,

THE SEASONS.

Miss Henrietta Beebe, Soprano.

Mr. H. S. Hilliard, Tenor.

Mr. George Prehn, Bass.